Simply Ageless

Alessia Davi

BALBOA.PRESS
A DIVISION OF HAY HOUSE

Balboa Press books may be ordered through booksellers or by contacting:

Balboa Press
A Division of Hay House
1663 Liberty Drive
Bloomington, IN 47403
www.balboapress.com
1 (877) 407-4847

Because of the dynamic nature of the Internet, any web addresses or links contained in this book may have changed since publication and may no longer be valid. The views expressed in this work are solely those of the author and do not necessarily reflect the views of the publisher, and the publisher hereby disclaims any responsibility for them.

The author of this book does not dispense medical advice or prescribe the use of any technique as a form of treatment for physical, emotional, or medical problems without the advice of a physician, either directly or indirectly. The intent of the author is only to offer information of a general nature to help you in your quest for emotional and spiritual well-being. In the event you use any of the information in this book for yourself, which is your constitutional right, the author and the publisher assume no responsibility for your actions.

Any people depicted in stock imagery provided by Getty Images are models, and such images are being used for illustrative purposes only. Certain stock imagery © Getty Images.

Scripture quotations taken from The Holy Bible, New International Version® NIV® Copyright © 1973 1978 1984 2011 by Biblica, Inc. TM. Used by permission. All rights reserved worldwide.

Print information available on the last page.

ISBN: 978-1-9822-4857-4 (sc)
ISBN: 978-1-9822-4859-8 (hc)
ISBN: 978-1-9822-4858-1 (e)

Library of Congress Control Number: 2020909754

Balboa Press rev. date: 05/27/2020

Contents

Author's Note   vii

Part 1: Going through Changes

Chapter 1   The Journey Begins   1

Chapter 2   More Than a Best Friend   5

Chapter 3   How to Survive High School   7

Chapter 4   Where Am I?   11

Chapter 5   What Does Love Have to Do with It?   13

Chapter 6   Don't Settle   15

Chapter 7   Rhythm Is a Dancer   17

Chapter 8   Faith   19

Chapter 9   Fight   23

Chapter 10   Inspiration   25

Chapter 11   A Random Act of Kindness   27

Chapter 12   Pretty Hurts   29

Chapter 13   Poem   31

Chapter 14   Law of Attraction   33

Chapter 15   Human Connection   35

Chapter 16   A Time for Everything   37

Chapter 17   Poems by Marissa Banks   39

Chapter 18   The 6-Phase Meditation by Vishen Lakhiani-
             Mindvalley   41

Part 2: The Power of You

Chapter 19   Awareness   49
Chapter 20   The First Step   57
Chapter 21   The Wall   63
Chapter 22   In Between   89
Chapter 23   A Star Is Born   109

Author's Note   131

Author's Note

Dear Reader,

The universe has just handed you a remarkable gift by allowing you to pick this book without you even knowing it. It's a very simple explanation. You see, we are all connected to the same source, whether it's God that you believe in, or something else. However, what doesn't change is the fact that we are all connected to one another, which is why even though there are millions of books out there, it was this particular one at this particular moment in time that has led you to start seeing the world in a whole new light. Whether or not you are going through a beautiful time here on earth, it doesn't matter. This book will allow you to see life with a new pair of eyes that you never knew you had. Recalling the metaphor, you must walk into another person's shoes to realize his or her actions. Well, you are about to walk into my size five feet that I assure you're going to want to take off many times, but you won't because my experiences will allow you to go out and metaphorically, or even physically, buy a new pair of size five shoes. God blessed me with a gift at about age five once I started seeing the world differently than most people, and I waited until I overcame my struggle with anxiety to tell you all about it, which you will read in part 2.

Thank you for choosing me to get you the life you never knew you could have.

Part 1

Going through
Changes

Chapter 1

The Journey Begins

Most people don't remember being born; all they remember is growing up. But my birth was a little different. I was born just under two pounds at St. Joseph's Hospital, where every person in my family was born. Aside from being a twin, which is the greatest thing that has ever happened to me, I was born unable to breathe fully, with a hole in my heart, and my organs deficient. From what my parents tell me, I was in and out of the hospital for about five years. I went through tests, being in an incubator, and having asthma issues—the works. Also, I know I was written about in medical books and on the news, so I guess you can say I am already famous. I have been a tremendous fighter because I wasn't even supposed to be alive today.

Because of this, I've always seen life in a way that is different than most people—whether it was in school, at work, at prom, or walking on the sidewalk. You see, my gift is that I can see and hear everything that people are going through, as well as feel their emotions, as if I am going through what they are experiencing. I've always had a huge heart and am able to find the good in absolutely everyone, even those who treated me poorly. Most important, in a room full of people, I am always drawn to the person who is alone or different or struggling with something; these people don't even have to tell me they're struggling. The only other person who I've met like this is Teresa, my spiritual healer. I thank God every day for this gift because his miracles are working through me to heal others with my words and actions.

I was bullied a lot about my height from first grade through seventh grade. Yes, I am four feet nine, which is not average, but I am still taller than a fire hydrant. If you have ever been picked on or bullied, you know how awful it feels. It feels like your heart is numb, like you simply want to be invisible, and like the whole world is crashing down. I don't know your experience with bullies, but mine was no walk in the park from the name calling, staring, and talking behind my back as if I couldn't hear them. Yes, it hurts, and you're probably wondering why I haven't said anything or fought back. It's because I have never been that type of person. But here's my advice, if you have ever been bullied by someone or know someone who has: it's time to take a stand because humans can be very cruel, and it needs to stop. Unfortunately, I have almost committed suicide because of it. Luckily it didn't happen to me, but I know for some people, it actually has. I want you to read these words very carefully: You can change someone's life in an instant with just one word, so please, for the sake of all those who have died, say something.

I will enlighten you with two bullying experiences that I truly don't wish upon my worst enemy. Let me paint a picture for you. I was in grade seven in Mr. Guillmen's class, and I was listening to the math lecture. I knew I had to go to the bathroom, but all of the sudden, I laughed, and the next thing I knew, I pooped in my pants. Can you believe it? I was walking around the whole day with poo in my pants. Lord knows how much I got made fun of that day. The worst part was not even that I smelled. It was then that I realized the indecency of humanity on that exact day because not one person had the courage to tell me that I smelled. So you can understand my frustration, knowing this happened and seeing the reaction on people's faces, not one person came up to me that day. That was when I discovered the true essence of the human soul: it's sometimes made up of a dark spirit that watches people suffer. I laugh now, but that whole day, I was trying to figure out why nobody said anything. To this day, I don't have the answer and probably never will. But no matter how traumatizing that was, I picked myself back up. After crying my eyes out, the next day I went to school and looked every classmate in the eye as if nothing had happened.

Then flash forward to grade eight, my first Halloween party. Did I say Halloween party? Well, here's another story for you. I showed up to the party dressed as a clown, with clown shoes, a clown face, and a horn, and my sister was dressed as Aunt Jemima I guess my sister and I, and two other people, didn't get the memo because everyone else was dressed but not in kids' costumes. It was my first and last Halloween party, let me tell you. After spending the night on a couch looking like a fool and watching everyone else in the room make out, dance, and get on the grinding train— yes, it was a thing—I realized how difficult life could be.

However, grade eight wasn't all that bad because I joined a youth group, put on some passion plays, and found my calling to worship Jesus Christ and God. Most important, I developed a stronger relationship with my sister, Christina.

Chapter 2

More Than a Best Friend

Growing up with my twin sister has been incredible, to say the least. Yes, we've had some fights and moments where we wanted to kill each other, but I would kill for her anytime. Imagine growing up with someone who was in the womb with you, who has kept you alive when you were literally dying in an incubator, who would be right there to pick up the pieces. Well, that's my sister for you. My sister, Christina, is out of this world. She is more than a best friend—she is my life in one human being. Without my sister, I wouldn't be living here today, I wouldn't be where I am today, I wouldn't be accomplishing this book, I wouldn't be in university, and I wouldn't have the confidence to express my opinions. I think you get the picture. She is the only person whom I can just look at, and she knows whatever I am feeling. My sister is the only person on this planet who has been through everything with me—my first kiss, my first date, my first boyfriend, my first driver's license, my first bully, my first breakup, my first job— the list goes on. My sister has been through every monumental moment that I have had in my twenty-two years of living.

I am writing this about her because I want you to think about that one person in your life and how much he or she has impacted you. Think about that one person who makes you smile and who gives you strength when times are tough. That one person who is there for you to tell you it's going to be okay, or to metaphorically push you on stage when you're too nervous to perform. So I am saying, Thank you, Christina. And for those who haven't found that person yet, well, I am here for you, and I won't have a problem pushing you to fight your inner battles.

Chapter 3

How to Survive High School

Well, there's no easy way to put this other than high school sucks. Let me rephrase that: being a student in high school sucks. I wish someone had given me tips on how to survive before I entered that place, but I wasn't given any, so that's why I am telling this to you. Whether you are going to high school soon or are already in it, you can relate. If anyone thinks ninth grade is tough, wait until you get to eleventh grade, when all of the real pressures come along. Let me walk you through my high school experience.

As a twin, I wasn't exactly a nobody because everyone knew me as one of the Davi twins, but I wasn't exactly popular either. Going into ninth grade was one of the most awkward experiences because I didn't know what crowd I fit into. Was it the drama crowd, the art crowd, the nerd crowd, the popular crowd, or the extras? Because I didn't know, I decided to get to know every crowd, and before I knew it, I knew pretty much everyone. Nonetheless, I played it safe until tenth grade, when I decided to try to become popular by going to almost every sweet sixteen, hall party, and house party—you name it. It got worse from there. There was not only jealously, regret, rebellion, and peer pressure, but there was more drama than one episode of *Gossip Girl*. I am so glad that part of my life is over now. The one thing I can say, though, is that I wish I had stayed myself. I was always trying to be someone my so called friends wanted me to be. I was always trying to get people to like me—and I still do, which is one of my biggest problems. The consequence of focusing so much on what people thought about me was that I forgot who I was and what I wanted. To this day, I am still trying to figure it out. And I have the biggest insecurity known to humankind but who doesn't?

Going for my driver's license was a roller coaster as well, because I didn't realize how long it was going to take me. G1 was the easiest thing to get and then after failing my G2 the first time, I thought to myself, Brush it off. Everyone fails the first time. I went again, and guess what? I failed. Now, you're really going to laugh: it wasn't until my eleventh try that I finally got my G2. In my defense, I think it was the evaluators because every time they would come into my car there was always something that happened right before me. Did I mention I have the worst luck in the world? Well, I do. I still remember the eighth time I did my test. This guy was swearing and yelling at the evaluator and played the race card, saying he can't even see because he's Asian. Of course, he got into my car after, and the rest was history for me. I've never had such a short driving test in my entire life. Anyway, by the eleventh try, I think the evaluator felt sorry for me and just gave me my license. I guess I can say I am a better driver for it today but, wow what an experience. Now to grade 11, it was kind of boring since all of the peer pressure of alcohol, drugs, and sex was already brought to my attention.

But the stressful part began when students started getting early acceptance letters to universities which I hadn't even applied to yet, let alone been accepted. The dreadful part was that I had to start thinking about my career and what I wanted to do with my life. Then I started thinking about well-paying jobs because I figured it was all about the money, as my dad would say. I searched and searched and came across the top three well-paid professions, which were no surprise: a doctor, a lawyer, or a veterinarian. I knew I was doomed because I didn't like math, science, or cats, so I came to the conclusion that the university I went to would choose my career for me.

Finally, we come to the end of high school, and it was prom season. Prom sucked. The music was awful, my dress was too long because I was four feet nothing, and the dress was too tight. My feet were killing me from the heels, and I didn't exactly have a prom date. The only thing that was good about it was the after-party, which was in a hotel the next day. But who cared? The dreadful four years of my life were finally over, and it was off to the next chapter of my life: university. Yikes.

Chapter 4

Where Am I?

As soon as I stepped into York University, I kept thinking to myself, *Where am I? Is this even a normal place? Why are people in pajamas during exams? Why did I just spend a thousand dollars on five textbooks? Why has my waist doubled in size? Why are there lectures the size of my entire house? Why do I even go here? Does this forty-year-old dad sitting next to me even go here?* I still can't answer those questions, and I probably won't be able to for the rest of my life, but I currently finished my fourth year and am going on to my fifth year of school, and let me tell you, the broke struggle is real. I wish I could give you some advice as to how to survive university, but there's no easy way to say that every day is like survival of the fittest. You're surviving to keep your grades, you're surviving not to fail, you're surviving to try to work, and you're surviving to get through the dreadful exams.

But I can tell you this from my experience: the only thing that has gotten me through this stressful time was 4:00 p.m. to watch Ellen's TV show. Ellen's whole story about struggling with finding herself related to me a lot. If I even meet her, I will say, "Thank you for pushing me through the rough times in my life." Another thing that has pushed me through the rough times is one of my favorite quotes by William Shakespeare: "Some are born great, some achieve greatness, and some have greatness thrust upon them." Who's to say that you can't achieve anything you want in life? To quote Ariana Grande, "If you want it, go get it." If you want a house, go buy it; if you want the most expensive car, go get it; if you want to have a boyfriend or girlfriend, go get one; if you want to get married, go to Vegas. Whatever you want to do, you can do it. My dad has always told me input equals output, so work hard, and you can achieve anything. Also, try to not be afraid of going for your dream. If you're afraid of university or college, you should go anyway. If you are afraid to tell someone you like him or her, you should do it anyway. If you're afraid to go camping you should go anyway. Whatever you're scared of, you should face it because God gave us one life, so why waste it?

This is the point in the book where I can hear my mom and dad saying, "You should practice what you preach," or, "I told you so." Honestly, I am guilty and can call myself a hypocrite because sometimes I am afraid of life and run away when times get tough, but who doesn't? If life was easy, then we would be all rich like the Kardashians. Do you think Einstein found it easy creating all of his theories? Do you think Bill Gates became one of the richest men in the world because it was easy? Nothing in life is easy.

Now, for those romance lovers out there, this next chapter is for you.

Chapter 5

What Does Love Have to Do with It?

Well, this is something that is close to my heart. I don't know why I love the concept of love or why I feel that when two people are in a relationship, it is the greatest thing on this planet. Even though I had my fair share of dates and relationships, I could never call that one person mine like my parents and grandparents have. The one thing I find fascinating is how much people nowadays want lust. Does that mean that love doesn't really exist?

I am no philosopher or expert on the subject matter, but I still feel that love today has to be strong for it to be real. Speaking as a young adult, all these guys today want only one thing, and if you don't put out, there is no such thing as love. So let me ask you this: How come people found love without requiring the statement "down to fuck"? What about something simple, such as my mom not having sex until she was on her honeymoon, or at least close to her wedding? Having said that, does love really have anything to do with it anymore? Or is it just some big infatuation that everyone thinks is love?

All I know for a fact is that we are all born with soul mates, and those soul mates will provide you with a lesson of either how to be in love or what to avoid. Regardless, love really does conquer all evil, is true, and is patient and kind. That's why I am full of love, and so are you.

Chapter 6

Don't Settle

One of my dad's favorite sayings is, "Why should I settle for the steak when I have a cow at home?" To this day, I don't even understand what he means, but all I can say is, Don't settle for just anybody or anything. Always aim high in life. If you want to teach, do it; if you want to get your master's degree, do it; if you want to go skydiving, do it. If you want to make a discovery, what are you waiting for? Nothing is stopping you from doing that. God put us on this earth, and it's not easy to say, "I am going to go skydiving tomorrow," but if it's one of your goals in life, nothing should stop you. Nothing should stop you from going to Italy or Spain or anywhere you want to go. My sentiment has always been "Never let the fear of striking out keep you from playing the game" (*A Cinderella Story*). Always strive to give something your all, even if you might fail. Never say never, find something you're good at, and go for the home run. Life is not meant to hide in the dark or shadows. If you're short like me, make everyone see you as if you were ten feet tall. Accomplish greatness by waking up tomorrow and doing something extraordinary.

Chapter 7

Rhythm Is a Dancer

Music is the definition of perfection. It gets you through every mood you are in. For instance, if you are happy, you listen to "Happy" by Farrell Williams. If you are sad, you listen to Ed Sheeran or Adele. If you are angry, you listen to any rock song. If you are in love, you listen to Taylor Swift. If you don't know how you are feeling, you can turn on the radio, and it will instantly put you into some kind of mood. Keep in mind that if you don't know the artists I just mentioned, you can listen to any type of artist to fulfill any mood. There is no judgment when it comes to music. Well, there's one judgment: if you don't like Beyoncé, then you need to get your hearing checked. I'm just saying.

Not only can you turn to music for help, but it allows you to escape to something greater than yourself. My piece of advice, wherever you are, is to just listen to music. Whether it's at work, school, the gym, your grandmother's house, or your backyard, put your headphones in and listen to a song. Trust me: you can feel instantly at ease. Music speaks every language and truly captures the soul. Music is the escape to this crazy world we live in, and it's the only thing that you can truly relate to and understand who you are as an individual. It's the rhythm that moves us and assures us that we are not alone, even if we feel it.

Another piece of advice is to sing out load and make everyone hear you. It actually feels amazing! Most of all, I encourage you to go to a concert; whether you are in the balcony seats or in floor seats, it takes you to a different place with people whom you share something in common with. You feel at ease that there are thousands of other people in the stadium with whom you can vibe. Trust me, it's the only place where you can sing really badly because, let's face it, everyone else is singing the same way.

Chapter 8

Faith

When you are feeling low, tired, sad, angry, or desperate, take a moment and say a prayer to God. From my experience, you are letting out how horrible you feel to the most powerful spirit in the world. God not only listens but answers in the most powerful way known to humankind. It may not be in that moment, the next day, or even the next week, but when it is answered, you know it and feel at ease. Follow this up with two simple words: "Thank you."

Speaking as a religious person, God has always been there for me. He gives me strength I never even knew I had. Even if you are not religious and have never said a prayer in your life, when you are feeling your lowest, simply lift your hands up and pray. I've had my fair share of moments where I lost faith, but God always knew I didn't mean it. God hears all, sees all, and does all in ways that will surprise you. Unfortunately, we have to be patient for the things we want most in life, like love or money. But I find that God gives us that patience somehow. God knows the path that we are set on, and we have to trust in it, we have to believe in it, and we have to imagine it.

Here's a little piece of advice: whatever you are going through right now in this stage of your life, it will pass. I don't know when, but I do know it will. For me, I have a lot of struggles within myself that I am very insecure about, and I don't know when it will go away. All I know is only God knows when my struggle will be solved.

I'm not going to lie to you: waking up every day is a struggle. It's a struggle to get out of bed and know that I have this burden on my shoulders, but I have to trust that God is here and will fix it. For all of you right now who are at your lowest point, God will help you. Trust me. I know it's frustrating, and I know you want to crawl into a closet and never open the door, but you have no choice. With every darkness, there is light at the end of the tunnel. God knows where you are meant to go and what your purpose is. So in the darkest times, simply say, "Only God knows," and, "Let go and let God."

This chapter is devoted to you, God. I love you and believe in you with all my heart. I am here to worship and bow down to you. Also, thank you, Jesus, for sacrificing your life so that everyone on this whole planet is able to be alive today. The Bible verse that resonates with this teaching is Revelations 21:4, "He will wipe every tear from their eyes. There will be no more death or mourning or crying or pain, for the old order of things has passed away." This is why every time I have tears rolling down my face, I know that God is right there to wipe them away.

Here is a special thanks prayer that I say to God because I wouldn't be here if it wasn't for him.

Dear God,

Thank you for another day to be alive and well. Thank you for allowing me to walk outside without needing assistance. Thank you for allowing me to go to the washroom. Thank you for allowing me to have a house and clothes to stay warm. Thank you for my supportive family that is always here for me when I need someone to talk to. Thank you for allowing me to spread kindness to those who do me wrong. Thank you for allowing me to take the high road even though I have so many negative things that I want to say back. Thank you for allowing me to see the beauty of life in all forms, including the birds outside, the trees, the sky, the sun, the moon, and all other living creatures here on earth. Most of all, thank you for allowing me to be your daughter; it's truly the best gift that I have ever been given.

Amen

Chapter 9

Fight

To all those who want to give up, to all those that can't sleep, and to all those who are endlessly fighting: I tell you to keep fighting. Never stop fighting for what you believe in, whether it's love, happiness, health, intelligence, beauty, a career, or absolutely anything. Don't give up. Speaking as a fighter since birth, I can assure you that it's worth it in the end. Never stop fighting for what you believe in. I challenge you to go out in this world and accomplish whatever it is that you want. Don't stop until you get it. God gave us this one life, meaning we have to live it to our best ability. That means you have to keep striving for what you want. Inspire people with your gift, and inspire people with all of your weaknesses. Never let anyone or anything stop you from fighting.

I am devoting this chapter to fighting because I often lack the patience and strength to fight for what I want. It's easier said than done, but you have to keep that fight in you. I want you to prove all the haters wrong. I want you to be more successful than you have ever been. I want you to never quit because as the saying goes, "Quitters never win, and winners never quit." My dad is probably shaking his head in dismay because I have just used another one of his lines. Yes, Dad, you're right as always.

Persevere, strive, and prove yourself wrong regarding your doubts. Think it, imagine it, and just do it. I write this for all those who are doubting themselves or are in the midst of giving up, because you need to read this. You need to read that you can do it. You can do it! Whoever you are, you can do it. I wish someone would have told me this a long time ago because it's hard to find someone who pushes you to your very best. There are many people in this world who want to see you fail, want to see you hurt, want to make you cry, want to be ahead of you. This is where you have the advantage over them: you have me. I'm here to tell you that you can and you will. I bet you didn't know that *impossible* really spells *I'm possible*. Well, you do now, so get out there and show yourself the possibility of what you can do. Be a fighter! Win the battle! Take home the gold medal!

Chapter 10

Inspiration

Whether it is Martin Luther King, Rosa Parks, God, celebrities, your parents, your friends, or your neighbors, I encourage you to look for inspiration from somewhere. At the end of the day, all these people who have inspired you were once inspired by someone or something. That's how they became the kind of people they were. I will bet you a million dollars that if you find that person or thing that gets you inspired, you will feel like the world is a better place. You will feel that there are endless possibilities for you, whether it's watching a movie or listening to a song or reading a book (hint, hint). Once you are inspired, I assure you that it will push you to wake up in the morning, and it will push you to go to school or work, walk the streets, go dancing—the list goes on.

I will fill you in on a little secret. My inspiration consists of God, my sister, my grandparents, my best friends Luca and Matthew, my cousin Cassandra, my Zia Franca, and my parents. It's not that the rest of the people in my life are not important. It's simply that these particular people have shown me how to live my life in different ways. God has inspired me to slay people with kindness. My sister has inspired me to lighten up in the most difficult situations, and if you know my sister, you know that there's not a day that goes by that she will not make you laugh.

My grandparents have inspired me with the most important life lesson of all, and that is to eat. Many of you are probably wondering why this is the most important lesson. Think about it. Eating brings people together, eating keeps us alive, and eating is something that you have in common with every single human and animal, which makes you feel that you are a part of the world and not just a speck of dust.

The next two people are by far the most amazing people I have ever encountered in my life, and not only because they are twins but because Luca and Matthew have shown me my self-worth. Their high energy has inspired me to love life as much as they do and to not settle for cheap things, because my presence deserves the expensive things. My cousin Cassandra has taught me how to get over my anorexia, my first heartbreak, and even my first suicide attempt. My Zia Franca has taught me how to love, and her love is the most powerful because it is through her hugs that she assures me everything will be okay.

To end the list, my parents have inspired me to be nothing less than my absolute self. My dad has taught me to not care about the little things like a pimple, a smell, or a bad hair day. My mom has taught me how to show the world what I am capable of by always reminding me that I have a lot to offer in this world, and she was right.

Go out there and get inspired so that you too can inspire people. Make a difference in this world, let the world know exactly who you are, and inspire people. You can change someone's whole life—that's how powerful the people in my life are.

Chapter 11

A Random Act of Kindness

I don't care what time it is. Whether you are reading this at 6:00 a.m. or 12:00 a.m., I want you to accomplish a random act of kindness to someone. Go through the drive-through of Tim Hortons and buy someone a coffee, or pay for someone's order. Give a homeless man a dollar, pick someone's pen up, have lunch with someone who is eating alone, hold the door for someone— the list is endless. I want you to be kind to someone today and do one thing for someone else. Give back to someone today. It can even be the act of praying for someone who needs it. I want you to take one moment of the day and be selfless.

I often don't realize how many times a day I think about myself. What I am doing? What do I need to do? Where do I need to go? What do I have to eat? When do I have to work out? But if I take one moment of the day to do something for someone else, it feels incredible. Think about it. We share this life with billions of other people, and all we do for twenty-four hours of every day is think about ourselves. It only takes that one moment to make someone's day, so stop the selfishness and start being selfless.

Chapter 12

Pretty Hurts

In the words of Beyoncé, "Pretty Hurts." I encourage everyone to do yourself a favor and go one day without fixing your hair, putting on makeup, tweezing your eyebrows, clipping your fingernails, shaving, dressing up, or working out. I encourage you to take one day and let it all hang out—literally "wake up like this." There is so much pressure on looking a certain way, dressing a certain way, and hiding behind our natural beauty. Well, I say fuck it. Today, I am not hiding behind eyebrow pencils, mascara, foundation, tight shirts, working out, and counting calories.

Take a day off work or school for one day and just do you. Wear sweatpants and baggy shirts, eat chips or cookies, watch movies, and go on an adventure for the day as you are dressed. Go on a walk in your pajamas. Do whatever you want. The best part is that the next day, you can beautify yourself again, knowing that you were your absolute self for one whole day. If you have no eyebrows, show them. If you have rolls on your stomach, embrace it for the day. If you drink a little too much, buy Advil the next day. I want you to take one day and be your absolute self. It feels like that weight on your shoulders has been lifted dramatically. Feel comfortable in your skin because you are beautiful. You are beautiful just the way you are. Those who tell you differently are jealous because they didn't have the nerve to do it themselves. It's time to metaphorically put on your birthday suit and show the skin you are in.

Do you remember the first time you came out of your mother's womb? You didn't even know what a mirror was until probably the age of three. Pretend as if you were that little boy or girl again and wake up in your own skin—not with fake eyelashes, girdles, or a comb through your hair. Also, take a selfie of your beautiful face and keep it on your phone to remind yourself of your inner beauty. If you really want to prove yourself worthy, post it on Instagram, Twitter, or Facebook and put the hashtag #Iwokeuplikethis. It doesn't matter how many likes you get; you know that society is not winning for one day, and you embrace the skin you were born in.

Chapter 13

Poem

One of my favorite things to do on a daily basis is read poems or prayers. Having said that, I thought I'd share with you the best poem ever written. This poem is called "Love Is Patient."

Love is always patient and kind.
It does not envy, it does not boast,
it is not proud.
It is not rude, it is not self-seeking,
it is not easily angered,
it keeps no record of wrongs.
Love does not delight in evil
but rejoices with the truth.
It always protects, always trusts,
always hopes, always perseveres.
Love never fails.
(1 Corinthians 13:4)

The thing about this poem is every time I read it, it's as if I am reading it for the very first time. The words behind it could not be more than the truth, which is why it is that powerful. If you read between the lines, it is saying that love is unconditional, and there is nothing greater than when you love someone or something because you accept all of them. You accept their flaws, you accept their anger, you accept their entire being, and you accept that within yourself, you know that there is no one else on this planet you can love more. Most important, it is saying that love never gives up on what it wants, even if the person doesn't love the other back. With love, every evil, every pain, every suffering, and every wrong is overcome instantly.

Chapter 14

Law of Attraction

According to *The Secret*, I have been living my life all wrong. Now, you're probably saying, "I want to know what this secret is." Well, first of all, it's a book and three simple words: law of attraction. These are the three simple words that I am living by right now. I wasn't sure how I was going to get over the struggle I am dealing with until I discovered *The Secret*. All you have to do is ask, believe, and receive. Somehow it will attract to you. I don't know how, I don't know how long it will take, and I don't even know when or where, but all I can say is it will. Whatever it may be, ask for it; whether it is a health issue, a relationship, or a car, simply ask for it.

Here's the catch: You can't ask it again because it simply won't work. Also, in order for it to come true, you have to believe in it, you have to imagine it, and you have to see it come into your life. You have to have faith that the universe will bring it to you. Then the law of attraction will instantly bring it to you somehow. I will surely keep you informed when this certain thing happens for me that I have asked for, but as of right now, I am trusting that the universe will bring it to me. I am trusting that my life will work itself out according to my feelings and intentions, and I encourage you to do the same.

Wherever you are reading this chapter, ask, believe, and receive. Then see what happens. I believe it will come true for you as it will for me. I am sending you all my love and faith in your intentions. Now it's your turn.

Chapter 15

Human Connection

I am no philosopher, but I believe that humans are connected one way or another. I believe that when you talk to someone, you either feel connected with them or you don't. For some people, it's rare to have a connection, and at other times it's not. Regardless, when you really connect with someone, it is something to hold on to because without even knowing it, that person gave you something that somehow will matter. Also, I believe that when two people are destined to meet, there is this connection that is so profound, it is as if a guardian angel granted you a miracle right before your eyes, even if you don't see that person again. In fact, I believe human connection is a mirror of fate, where the universe suddenly created this powerful occurrence for two people who are destined to be together to cross paths. Also, human connection can explain the reason how life can work out exactly the way you pictured it in your mind because it is a relationship you made with life. It is a feeling so powerful that only you can control.

To get further explanation, I discussed human connection, love at first sight, and destiny with a friend who, for the purpose of confidentiality, will remain anonymous. My friend said, "I believe in human connection, but I believe that the only way you can achieve it is to not force feelings." I took this to heart because for years, a lot of us are guilty of forcing feelings, whether it is toward lovers, family members, friends, or colleagues. But the beauty of human connection is that it is an indescribable connection based on intuition and mutual attraction. At the end of the day, I find that true love and relationships are unconditional and communicated through simple eye contact and expressions. The takeaway here is the person who you look at and feel the word *home* with is the person with whom you're going to spend the rest of your life.

Chapter 16

A Time for Everything

There is a time for everything.
There's a time for everything done on earth.
There is a time to be born. And a time to die.
There is a time to tear down. And a time to heal.
There is a time to cry. And a time to laugh.
There is a time to be sad. And a time to dance.
There is a time to scatter stones. And a time to gather them.
A time to hug. And a time not to.
A time to search. And a time to stop.
A time to keep. And a time to throw away.
A time to tear.
And a time to mend.
A time to be silent.
And a time to speak.
A time to love.
And a time to hate.
A time for war.
And a time for peace.

(Ecclesiastes 3:1–8 New International Version)

Chapter 17

Poems by Marissa Banks

The poems below by Marissa Banks are close to my heart because they truly resonate with many of my life experiences. I wanted to include them because I am sure you will find some sort of connection as well.

Nature is beautiful
Because it makes no effort
To be itself
The moon glows
The plum falls
And the nightingale sigs
Each following it's natural course
Without restraint
Or Regret
But Look
At Yourself
You too
Went from being nothing
To being vibrantly alive
Without doing a thing
So what makes you think you need to try so hard Now?

I watch you, Mind
Ricocheting back and forth
Throwing all of your magic tricks and cards about

Flailing and out of breath
Desperate to convince me why I need to
keep trying, moving, becoming.
But I already told you-
I'm happy with it all
Just the way it is.
Anyways, your velvet cape is tattered and your eyes look tired
And isn't the joy of winning a race
Really just the relief to re-catch your breath?
I wish you would believe me
And just sit down for a cup of tea.
I'd love for you to show me that trick with the Ace of Spades
Again.

Chapter 18

The 6-Phase Meditation by Vishen Lakhiani-Mindvalley

This meditation is incredibly profound because it allows you to connect with a powerful source that is found outside yourself. I am happy to say that I have tried it, and it allowed me to find my inner peace with not only myself but the world.

I want you to take a deep breath and as you exhale gently feel your body sinking into a relaxed state of mind. Use any regular meditation deepening or count down tool if used in the past to reach a deep level of mind. To help you go even deeper, I will gently guide you through a relaxation of your physical body. Feel your scalp relax, feel this relaxation gently flow to your forehead, now your eyes, feel your eyelids relax, feel that sensation of relaxation gently flow downward to your physical body. Move the feeling to your face, your neck, your shoulders now your upper arms, your hands, your chest, your abdomen, your knees, your calves, your feet, and feel that feeling of relaxation all the way down to your toes. Your now in a deep relaxed state of mind.

The first phase is to draw your attention to your consciousness, you most likely feel this consciousness in your head. Focus on this consciousness, feel that consciousness expand now to encompass your entire body. Picture it as a white light emanating your head and surrounding your entire body as a white bubble. Now picture this light emanating further surrounding and encompassing your entire room and anyone who may be in that room. A peaceful, calm and loving light. See it expand it even further and expand it to your entire home and feel the sensation of peace, love, joy resonating from you to anyone who may be in your home. Feel it expand further by imagining it in your neighborhood and know that you are connected to every living creature, plant, animal or human in this neighborhood. Feel this light expand even further and encompassing your city or town, now encompassing your state or region. Now your country, the continent, now feel this light emanating to the entire planet and feel yourself connected to the planet. See yourself for what you are, a piece of consciousness directly connected to every other life form on planet earth.

We now move on to phase two, gratitude. Bring to mind between five to 10 things that make you grateful, joyful, happy within the last 24 hours. If you can't think of anything within the past 24 hours expand it to the last 3 days, week, or month. Think about things that happened in your work or career, things that happened while you were traveling or your free time. Things that happened in your family life or with loved ones. It can be something big or something small like a nice big cup of coffee that you had in the morning. Express gratitude and the feeling of joy when these incidents occurred. I will give you a minute to list as many incidents of gratitude that you can think of and you can write them down if you want ... As you imagine and bring back to mind these incidents and moments make them as vivid as you can incorporate all five senses taste, sound, touch, smells and images. Most importantly, incorporate your emotions so that feeling of joy or happiness when you experience these moments. Feel that feeling of gratitude vibrate all throughout your body to head to your toes and know that when you express gratitude for beautiful moments in life you open the way for these moments to repeat themselves and grow in terms of their magnitude.

We now move on to phase three, removing negative charges. A negative charge is any negative feeling you may have towards a person or an incident. Bring to mind someone, anyone whom you had a negative charge with. A waiter that rubbed you the wrong way, a co-worker whom you had a disagreement with. A family member that you fought with. It can be big or it can be small. See that person in front of you about six feet away, see their face or their entire body. You will now say that you apologize for any wrong that you have brought to them whether it was talking bad about them behind their back or anything else that comes to mind. Know that on a deeper level we are all one and we are all connected and any negative charge towards any other living creature, person or life form is in a way a charge against ourselves and we must get rid of these charges. When you are finished expressing forgiveness to this person. Ask them to forgive you, imagine them forgiving you. Imagine that forgiveness moving toward you straight to your heart. Feel that feeling of calm and peace as you recognize that forgiveness is easy. When first starting out, practice this exercise where forgiveness is easy and repeat this exercise to as many people to whom you may have a negative charge within the last 24 hours or few days or week.

We now move on to phase four, visualizing your perfect future. For the next two minutes simply visualize different aspects of your life as they would unfold in the future. Keep in mind that as human beings we tend to overestimate what we can do in one year but, we tend to underestimate what we can do in three years. So take a three-year stance, see your life three years from now, see moments of joy, achievement, beauty, accomplishments, and success. Let this be a free flowing imagination exercises and remember to incorporate all five senses. What would your health and body look like three years from now? What does your family life look like three years from now? Who are your friends and how do you spend time with them? What new skills are you learning and absorbing? What acts of service are you contributing to the community and the world? What does your career look like? How do your finances look like? What new traits have you brought into your character? What beautiful experiences are you having to bring fun and adventure into your life? What does you love life look like? I will now give you a minute to move on and to take it into any direction that you wish again you can write it down if you like … Remember to incorporate all five senses make the day dream as vivid as possible. As you wrap up mentally tell yourself let this or something better unfold in my life.

We now move on to phase five in which you will visualize your perfect day. Ask yourself to let all the beautiful things I have dreamt about and written down come to me. How would my perfect day come to me and unfold? If you're doing this exercise in the morning visualize your perfect day when you leave the house today. If you're doing it at night visualize it starting in the morning when you wake up. See yourself having an amazing breakfast, a wonderful commute to work, see your work day unfolding, see friends and family coming into your life, see yourself having an amazing dinner with a special someone, watching your favorite TV show, reading a good book, watching a movie, working on a creative project, going to bed and having perfect sleep. I will give you a minute to see your day unfold from the time you wake up to the time you go to sleep in pure perfection in a way that will make you happy, grateful and let your day dream of your ideal self-three years from now come to you with ease begin now in which you can also write down … Make it as vivid as possible bring in emotions of joy, excitement, gratitude as you see your day unfolding. Bring yourself to the end of the day and see yourself going to bed and going into a deep, comfortable, rejuvenating sleep ready to start the next day and make that next day amazingly wonderful too.

We now move on to phase six, in this phase call upon any higher power that you believe in. May be a God, a saint, an avatar, an angel, a guide, it may be the force of light that emanates the entire world. It may be your own inner strength, your religion, your beliefs in atheism, or spirituality don't matter here. You are simply calling upon any higher power externally or internally that you believe in. Ask this higher power to bless you, to give you luck, energy, support and to help you craft your perfect day and make your dreams for the next three years unfold. This is because only when you are happy and when you are contributing to humanity can you provide happiness and contribute to others. Feel that support come down on you. Feel that beam of light hitting the scalp of your head and gently flowing downwards to your entire body, from your skull down to your spine, emanating in your torso, your chest, your arms, your legs. Feel this protective energy embracing you and know that luck is on your side and that the universe has your back. I will give you a few moments to feel this energy surrounding and supporting you. We will now come out of this meditation. I will now count from one to five at the count of five you will come out of this state of meditation and be ready to see your perfect day unfold. 1, 2, 3, at the count of five you will come out of this meditation feeling wonderful, rejuvenated, positive, optimistic, ready for that perfect day and ready to see your life in the next three years unfold in complete success. 4, 5 you have now come out of the six phase meditation. You know now that your day is about to start in a wonderful way and that all your wildest dreams and visions for the next three years are coming to you.

Part 2

The Power of You

Chapter 19

Awareness

The second part of this book is dedicated to mental health because I recently become aware that I had been diagnosed with it. To be mentally ill is not only from all of the thoughts that are going on in your head; it's the actions that follow it. Initially, I figured I had no social skills because I spent most of my time in a basement reading, but my psychologist will argue differently. I used to spend most of my days in thought, thinking about my past, thinking about my present, and thinking about the future. This may sound normal on paper, but trust me, it's not. I would wake up every day doing the same routine by eating breakfast, having a thought and obsessing over it, working out sometime in the day, and having a thought and obsessing over it. I would have dinner, have a thought and obsess over it, and go to bed to relive the cycle the next morning. I think you get the picture now. Compare this to a regular person who spends her day thinking but doesn't allow those thoughts to control her life. As for me, I was surrounded by four walls all day, every day, whether it was in the basement, a classroom, my psychologist room, my bedroom, or the bathroom.

I don't really know how I got there, but inevitably I felt stuck. I felt trapped in this mind that never stopped running over fears and negative affirmations. Throughout the rest of the book, I have added some of my diary entries from the past that are very personal to share. I feel they are necessary because I want people who are going through this to really connect with this book and feel that they are not alone. Therefore, the rest of the book is going to walk you through my life in the past, but you are able to practice these teachings in the very present.

October 3, 2016

Dear God,

Maybe you have a bigger plan for me than I may know. I am contemplating life right now. I just want things to be the way they were. I want to fall in love again, I want to feel beautiful, and I want to be liked by people. I'm very upset and angry that I am the way I am. I'm angry that I gave up on myself and that this beautiful, confident, sexy, good girl who didn't care about what people think and was at the highest point is not here anymore. God, I know I may have been not so close to you as I was in the past, but now I really need the opportunity to allow life to come to me again. I really need you to give me the opportunity to fall in love, to have an appearance of roses, to be happy, to have people like me, and to become the woman I am meant to be. Please take me in your hands and allow my life to come back. Father, you have always helped me since I was a little girl. I ask you at my most desperate time to create miracles for me, please. I know I am supposed to let go, but it's hard! It's very hard. My family's supporting me, and my therapist, whom I also pray for, is supporting me because she is in the process of helping me get better. I am very grateful that you have brought her into my life because she is an incredible women, and I pray that our bond may stay strong. However, God, I just pray that I become the woman I was meant to be. God, you are my only hope in the sense that I need more than just exercise, makeup, clothes, showering, food, water, shelter, and a family. I need a miracle. God, please help me. Please, with your one touch, help me, my body, and my spirit become a better woman. God, as a woman, I have needs, as you know, to be loved and to be confident and beautiful. Mother Mary, allow me to have your skin, your face, and your body. I love you, God and Mother Mary, till the day I die.

Amen

February 5, 2016

Dear God, thank you for the ability to have the confidence to talk to a guy. I want to thank you because you showed me what life really is and how special our decisions that we make are. God, I want you to know that I know I am not alone, and you showed me that today. You showed me that I can be something greater than a girl in the basement. I still put my faith in you unconditionally, and I pray for the chance at love. I love and praise you all the days of my life.

Amen

April 16, 2016

Dear God,

Just answer my prayers, please. I am becoming very impatient and frustrated. I don't know what to do. God, I am working out, I am eating healthy, and I am treating my body well. Please allow my thoughts to go away. Just please, Father, almighty God. I have needs, God. I just can't take this anymore. I pray for all those who are suffering. I pray for the good and the bad. I pray for all of it.

Amen

September 24, 2017

Dear God,

I don't think I have ever felt this alone in such a long time. Why can't I just be normal? I'm regretting my life. I have suicidal thoughts, I want to die, and I don't know why I am here. What is my purpose on this earth? Why don't I have anyone in my life? What is wrong with me? I am completely miserable, God. Please, you know me more than anyone else on this entire planet save me from this misery. Please, Lord, save me!

Amen

May 6 2017

Dear God,

I met a guy for a strange reason at this club tonight, and his name is Nick. I never felt so good to know that someone accepts me for all of me. Is this happening, is it real, is it a movie? I actually don't know. All I know is this feeling is incredible. Thanks!

Amen

August 7, 2017

Dear God,

You know the guy I was telling you about. Well, I'm his girlfriend now, but something feels off, and I don't know what it is. Is it me? Give me a sign. I feel like I am not myself. I feel that this relationship is going nowhere. What the hell is wrong with me? I don't know.

Amen

May 15, 2017

God, something horrible happened. I broke up with Nick, and my whole life is a mess. I can't think straight, I am having panic attacks in the middle of the night, and I am a complete disaster. Why did I let him go? Besides the fact that he didn't come to my birthday, didn't buy me a present, and didn't celebrate our anniversary at a restaurant. I feel like I am all alone now, more than ever. Will I ever find love again? I highly doubt it. Who wants to be with this fucked-up mind of a person?

P.S., Sorry for swearing.
Amen

August 17, 2018

Dear God,

I have such a bad relationship with my father and mother. I am so mad at them. Probably because I am mad at myself. Why am I so selfish? Why am I so flustered? Why do I want to fall in love so badly? Why do I want to have these feelings go away? Why have I been doing drugs and drinking so much? Why can't I love myself? I can't seem to love the person Alessia. I just want a guy to fight for me, treat me right, make me feel like a queen, and accept me for me. I couldn't go to work again today. I feel very insecure; it hurts.

Amen

This now brings us to September 7, 2018, and I am lost for words at the diary entries I have just disclosed. It was really rough to share that with all of you, but I did it. However, the next chapters will describe to you what I am doing on a daily basis regarding my mental health so that it can possibly be used as your process as well.

Chapter 20

The First Step

The first step I decided to take is see a psychologist. This is my first day seeing her, and let me tell you, she reminds me exactly of my sister, which is why I am completely in love with her. Not lesbian in love, because I am straight, but love like a family member. She has curly hair, is full of confidence, is not afraid to interrupt me when I am speaking. and has this angelic presence about her.

We first started talking about why I came here in the first place, and surprisingly I was able to tell her everything. I told her how I feel alone, and I told her how I am unaware of who I am. When she asked me about my fears, I was a little hesitant but told her anyway. I told her I am afraid of hugging people, I am afraid of not finding love, I am afraid to go outside, I am afraid to leave the house, and I am afraid to be in public places. You name it, and I said it. I told her how I was afraid of people not liking me and how I am afraid of losing myself even more.

Then we talked about my past, such as relationships or past experiences with guys. This really hit me hard because I had to talk about my almost rape experience. I feel that if I told her, I can tell all of you, so here it goes.

One night I was in the parking lot at school, in a car with a guy who will remain anonymous. We were making out, nothing crazy. When I asked if I could open the door, he immediately locked it. I then tried to open the door again, and he kept pushing the lock shut. I said, "I don't want to do this anymore. I want to go home," but he didn't listen and put his body on top of me, making it harder for me to get out. I tried once more to open the door, but he wouldn't let me open it. I didn't scream, I didn't shout, and I didn't yell. I tried to get him off of me so I could get out of the car. On the tenth try, I got out, and he drove me home. Looking back at it now, I was so stupid, and I am still traumatized to this day. How could I let a guy do that to me? All I know is talking about it brings tears to my eyes because all the memories came back, and his face immediately came in my mind.

After I told my psychologist, I then talked about my anxiety and how it is always showing up for me, even if my thoughts are not true. At the end of our session, she left me with three things I have to do before I go see her, which is go outside to three places; it doesn't matter where they are. I did two so far: I went to school, and I went to Walmart, which were both very bad experiences because I haven't been around people in a while. Hopefully, I make some progress next week. Wish me luck.

August 8, 2018

Dear God,

It's boring old Alessia again. What did I do today? Well, I didn't talk, that's for sure. I didn't associate with any people whatsoever. But I learned something about myself. I began comparing myself to Macbeth and how he went into madness. Specifically, his famous "Is this a dagger which I see before me" (act II, scene I, line 33) made me realize that all of my thoughts are hallucinations, as if I was seeing a bloody dagger in the air. But like Macbeth, I can't seem to believe that those thoughts are not real. Am I going to be stuck like this forever? Am I going to walk the face of this earth in my head twenty-four seven? Am I going to die like this" I sincerely hope there is some kind of miracle or epiphany that is going to happen.

Amen

September 10, 2018

I have written a poem today. I didn't actually know I wanted to write a poem until I picked up a pen and paper. But I just knew I had to write down my feelings. So I wrote.

> I lay in this bed all alone,
> Waiting just to be shown
> Does anyone realize I am here?
> Why am I constantly living in fear?
> Who are you to judge that I am no good enough?
> Every day seems so tough.
> Why do I not want to exist?
> Yet still have the courage to persist.
> Can anyone hear me?
> Or am I just a little bee?
> Trying to ignore my presence
> As if there was no fluorescence.
> Only time will tell.
> In the meanwhile, I will just keep on regretting the day I metaphorically fell.
> And as for those who hate and doubt,
> I say, I am here to shout!

September 11, 2018

I went to my psychologist today and talked about my old habits, such as me smoking pot, my alcohol abuses, et cetera. But it's weird. I still feel like I am the only one in the universe alone. I feel like the only one who is out of place. I feel like the only one who wakes up in the morning and doesn't know who the fuck she is. Why is this happening to me? I am so discouraged to wake up in the morning. I am so discouraged to leave the house. I'm so discouraged to be alive right now. Is there a magical power that can possibly take this all away somehow? I don't know. I wish I did, though; it would make my life a lot easier.

So about my appointment. We then tried something new. It's called cognitive behavioral therapy, and basically our thoughts influence our behaviors on a daily basis, which influences our emotions. For example, a regular person who gets a flat tire will say, "Oh, well. I got a flat tire. I guess I have a day off work today." That person calls an Uber and feels at ease. However, my thought process is this: I get a flat tire. I am a wreck, I'm sweating, and I hyperventilate. I constantly say, "My life is over, it's done. This always happens. Another bad thing wrong with my day." This then leads to a probable panic attack and a trip to the hospital instead of the mechanic. Well, maybe it's not that extreme, but you get my point. This leads me to feeling depressed, sad, and lonely all over again. So yeah, that's my brain compared to a normal person. One thing is for sure: I am currently not getting any better.

As for my assignment this week, it is to write down all my activities of where I go, whether it is a walk around the block or Walmart, because I have to get out of the house more. I hope I can do it, but I highly doubt it because my life is a mess. One big activity after another. When is it going to get better? Why me?

Signed,

Lonely

September 16, 2018

A little update. I didn't go out this whole week, trapped inside four walls. I did my homework all weekend and felt empty as fuck. I miss smiling, I miss laughing, I miss my confidence, and I miss feeling like I can fly. Where is this light? Where is it in this dark room I am in? You never realize how good you have it until something unexpected hits you like a ton of bricks. I guess it is just not my time right now to feel good. I let myself go. I let myself go. And I am now just waiting for God's plan, as it is written in the Bible.

> "For I know the plans I have for you," declares the Lord, "plans to prosper you and not to harm you, plans to give you hope and a future." (Jeremiah 29:11)

Signed,

Anonymous (because I don't know who I am)

Chapter 21

The Wall

I started taking a mental health class at school as part of my elective so that I could relate my textbook knowledge to this book regarding my condition. Historically, I learned that people around the nineteenth century who were considered mentally ill were put in asylums surrounded by a wall so that they could be isolated from the city in which they lived. However, this wall acted as a barrier for the purpose that if you were considered mentally ill, you were no longer worthy of socializing with the rest of the world. I discovered that even though there is no physical wall that is isolating people who are mentally ill today, society still has this metaphorical wall put up in their heads regarding mental illness. It doesn't matter how much medication you take, how much therapy you seek, or how much group support you go to. People who suffer from mental illness will always be seen as different.

I say enough! It is time to tear down this wall that society keeps putting up. I don't understand why our society in which we live is not paying enough attention on mental health and educating more students regarding this issue, because it can help save several lives. As for me, it is saving mine through reaching out to people and understanding that I am not alone. In order to tear down this wall, we need to have increased support groups, employment opportunity programs for people who suffer from mental illness and can't seem to hold a job down, greater entertainment regarding mental health, and adequate housing. I repeatedly state the obvious: that I am surrounded every day with this barrier.

Thus, in order to change this stigmatism, I started taking action by asking people on Instagram to share their experiences with mental health. Their stories in the next pages and throughout the rest of the book have inspired me to keep writing and should inspire you to take another look at life from a different perspective.

From @theshadeyouhide (aka Rebecca),

When I was 15, I was diagnosed with clinical depression. I spent my formative year's sulking, crying, begging God for a way out. I occasionally self-harmed and came up with many ways to kill myself—attempting few, succeeding in none. As the years went on, I found God, began to see a therapist and became very vocal in discussing my depression with loved ones. But, the thing is … depression never fully goes away. Earlier this year I went through another depressive episode. But, instead of spending weeks in my room isolated from everyone I'd only spend maybe a day inside my room. And instead of isolating myself entirely, I'd turn to my therapist or talk to a loved one. The point of me sharing this is that although my depression is never as bad as it was years ago, it is still something that I and many others constantly struggle with. September is National Suicide Prevention Month, and today I've decided to share my story in hopes that it can help at least one person. My advice to those struggling with depression/thoughts of suicide: I'm with you. I know the feeling of not wanting to wake up the next day, feeling miserable, misunderstood, and alone. But, please keep holding on. If you don't feel strong now, I promise you WILL. You've made it so far; keep choosing that spark of hope. I am with you.

To the rest of you: please check on your loved ones. Tell them you love them. Smile at strangers. Do random acts of kindness.

Listen to people when they say they're feeling down. You never know what someone is going through. A little goes a long way.

From bipolarbear,

If you want to kill yourself, stop and breathe for a hot minute. You are thinking irrationally. I know you probably think no one will care if you die, but they will. Remember when you were about to move back at Islington, and you and Jeremy were lying on the couch, and he told you that he loved you and every part of you. Your raw emotions drew his out. He said that you remind him of that girl from *Dragon Ball Z* that changes personalities whenever she sneezes, lol. You are different, and that isn't bad. He said at first he wanted you to be what he wanted, but he ended up falling in love with the person you grew into, and you grew together. You are loved. The other day. alias said she loves you and that you understand her and make her feel like she's not alone. and you have students that love you and look up to you, and your friends don't hate you; show me the proof. There's no proof that anyone hates you or is out to get you. Your friends love you. You and Claudine just started becoming friends, and you can tell her anything, and she gets you, and you get her in a way that no one else can because you've gone through the same life. Nadine is not even done growing yet. Don't you want to see her graduate? Don't you want to eventually forgive your mother, and see your father get better, and help your grandparents, and get married, and live in a house and have children? To eventually have a dream and change the world through love. You have so many reasons to live. Don't believe your brain; she is tricking you again. The pain is temporary, babe. Every time this happens, it always passes. Accept it, try to self-soothe until it passes. You are strong, and I love you so much love.

Letter from what my crazy ass is telling me, Jizzy Jazzy xx

From @noguts_nostory,

I read somewhere that the average human can process 150 relationships, and anything beyond that forces the brain to rationalize and guess. I wonder if the one we have with ourselves is among the 150, if it holds the same weight or influence. Mental health seems to be a topic everyone struggles with at some point, but very few of us have the balls/ovaries to have a conversation about it. We lived behind seemingly perfect Instagram posts and numb ourselves with a plethora of vices, anything to avoid how we truly feel.

Once upon a time, I was in a relationship with a man who was actively seeing a therapist and taking medication for anxiety, both equally important things that I was not made aware of. It didn't take long for us to hit a rough patch, but it also didn't take us long to get through it once these details were brought to light. I remember reacting with a soft laugh, followed by "That's it? That's the big secret? Here I thought you were going to tell me your favorite beer is Coors Light and that you hate dogs." It was a shock to hear that I was the first person whom he felt completely safe with, as I'm sure it was shocking for him to be met with acceptance and understanding.

I guess what I'm getting at is we're all battling something—internally, externally, worldwide. It's paramount that we don't remain bystanders, that we don't look the other way when the numbers in suicides and overdoses keep piling up. Don't just check in on your friends when you think they need it. Check in because it might be the only silver lining on the darkest of nights.

Reaching out to these incredible people inspired me to pay tribute to the people that our world has lost due to mental illness, so we can slowly prevent ourselves from encountering yet another funeral.

Mac Miller lost his battle with mental health on September 7, 2018, at the age of twenty-six.

Musician Tom Petty lost his battle with mental health on October 7, 2017, at the age of sixty-six.

Robin Williams lost his battle with mental health on August 11, 2014, at the age of sixty-three.

Lee Thompson Young lost his battle with mental health on August 19, 2013, at the age of twenty-nine.

Ivy League track star Madison Holleran, at the age of nineteen, lost her battle with mental health on January 17, 2014.

The famous artist Vincent van Gogh, at age thirty-seven, lost his battle with mental health by committing suicide on July 29, 1890.

Marilyn Monroe, at the age of thirty-six years, lost her battle with mental health on August 5, 1962.

The legendary Michael Jackson lost his lifelong battle with mental health on June 25, 2009, at the age of fifty years old.

Alexander McQueen, one of the best designers in fashion, lost his battle with mental health at the age of forty on February 11, 2010.

Lucy Gordon, Spiderman actress aged twenty-eight years old, lost her battle with mental health on May 20, 2009.

September 24, 2018

The word of the day is *triumphant*, meaning being a winner at something. I chose it because it's how I am feeling. For the first time, I didn't care what anyone thought about me, I didn't worry about people around me, and I didn't get overly anxious. That's why I am feeling triumphant today. I have overcome a great battle within myself to concentrate on the present moment, and it feels incredible. I actually talked to people, I was outgoing, I laughed, and I sat quietly without being disturbed about the thoughts that were going through my head. I don't know how I did it, but I did. Despite knowing my condition, despite knowing that the thoughts are true, and despite feeling uncomfortable, I actually did it.

Also, I got more DM messages on Instagram regarding people's battles with mental illness. I feel so blessed to know I am not alone and share people's experiences. Joseph's story and others have encouraged me to not give up and continue to feel powerful about my overall well-being, so thank you to everyone who is sharing this journey with me. I love you.

From @asensitiveman,

> He thought she was being overly dramatic. She was being extra. In reality, she was having a panic attack. This recently happened to my best friend … and I'm not violent by nature, but I wanted to send that dude's head spinning.
>
> "Extra" means being excessively dramatic or emotion for unnecessary reasons. Think some reality TV shows.
>
> When I first was dating my best friend, I didn't quite understand her behavior as well. I was excessive. It was a lot to take in. I'd never seen someone react that way, but I never thought it was unnecessary or faked. She genuinely was troubled mentally.
>
> Yes, the pain is in your head, but that doesn't make it any less real. She went through things most people couldn't imagine … And it is difficult

to process. Me too. When I talk with my friends about what happened to me, there is a disconnect because they don't understand. They don't know the feeling.

Don't let people define your mental state for you.

Also, remember that not everyone will understand what we go through. For the longest time, I didn't understand. Your loved ones might seem insensitive or distant, but it is usually because they don't get it.

I get it, though. In the past year, I have started having panic attacks. What has helped you deal with them? How do you handle people who seem insensitive? I could use the advice.

Signed,
#onebigokfamily

From, @kara_julia_,

I was 20 turning 21 when I was diagnosed with general anxiety disorder. I was given an antianxiety and a therapist for this. (I also suffer from depression, chronic migraines, and ADD.) School had just started, and it was my first time living on campus. Afraid of gaining my "freshman 15" as a sophomore, I signed up with a trainer at the edge in Hamden.

I was working out, and I changed to a healthy diet. A few months go by, and I have gained weight. Upset by this, I called my mom. We did some research and come to find out a side effect of the medication was weight gain (why the doctor thought giving someone with anxiety a medication with a weight gain side effect was a good idea, this is beyond me, lmao). By this time, I was 20 pounds overweight.

I slowly came off my meds, which lead me to a dark place. I didn't go to class, I was angry all the time, and above all else I was tired. So I packed my stuff to go home for the rest of the year.

Fast-forward 8 months later. I got my medicine regulated, got back down to 135 pounds, enrolled back in school, ended up on the dean's list, and became part of Active Minds on campus. Two years after that, I graduated.

I'm the happiest I've ever been. So believe me when I tell you, you can live your life with a mental illness if you don't let it control you. Yeah, easier said than done, lol. I still struggle sometimes; we all do.

Signed,
#Staystrong

From @tommy,

Smile. They say if you just smile, you'll become happier in yourself, and everyone around you'll be happier too.

Personally, I think that's bollocks. From someone who's known for being a bit of a smiler, they ain't all happy smiles. From someone who suffers from depression now and again, smiling is one of the hardest things to do. If you manage it, it's fake. When I've got to fake smile, it kills me on the inside, kills me for being false. Yes, I do it just to be polite, but most of the time it's just to put on a façade up of how you're really feeling, and you don't want to show it. It doesn't make you feel better; it makes you worse knowing you're going to have to be out there in public. Pretending to be fine mentally is so tough. You've got to fight with yourself in your own head to get out there and socialize when all you want to do is be left alone and cry.

So if you see someone smiling, don't look at their mouth; look into their eyes and see for yourself if it's genuine, or if there is something else going on. It'll mean so much to them if you're in doubt if they're being genuine or not, if they're okay. Not just a small talk kind of "You okay?" but meaningful questions of "Are you okay?" They won't ask for help. I'll never ask for help. That's probably the biggest factor why people get depressed, because they won't ask for help, and everything gets on top of them. I've personally been where they've been many times. I was there this weekend. It's rough mentally. You just break down crying, and you don't know why, and you've got to scratch, crawl, and climb to try to get out of

the black hole inside your head. I've had enough
of it.

Now I've realize it's time to talk before it gets
worse. I told my family this week what's going
on. They kind of knew something was wrong, so
when my sister asked, "You okay?" instead of the
"Yeah, I'm fine" answer I usually give, I took a
deep breath, argued with myself in my head for
a few seconds whether to tell the truth, and then
thought, *Fuck it—just tell the truth.* From that
moment, now I can see the light for a change,
not just the dark. My family have been rallying
around me and it's lifting the weight off slightly.
I'm not cured by all means, but I know it's going
to get easier from now on!

Signed,
#It's okay to say you're not okay

Tommy made me realize that it's okay to say you are not okay.
It means that you are getting the help you need. I want everyone
reading this right now to know that this book is not only for
those battling with mental illness, even though it's a big part of it.
This book is for those who have a secret they are struggling with
and need to let it out to someone. If you are gay and are afraid,
come out; you won't be judged by me. If you are confused, talk to
someone who will guide you to the path of wisdom. Don't make
something weigh on your shoulders for any longer. Trust me, once
you let your story out or tell someone what your inner battle is,
you will feel incredible. It's hard, believe me, but we need each
other. We need to create more peaceful situations for everyone.
There is not one individual who is perfect, so let's talk about our
imperfections one person at a time.

I hope with this book I encourage you to reach out, whether it is to me or to someone else, to find your inner happiness. Every day is a damn battle for me. One day I feel infinite, and then the next day I will feel bottomless. However, I do know that I can sleep one hour at night knowing I am creating a difference in this world through my writing. What's your talent? Go show the world what you've got. I created a motto for myself, "This will be my year," and I am going to stick by it until my book gets published and until I find true happiness. Having said that, this too can be your year.

From @Colby_grey,

For years, I never understood where I was supposed to get emotional help. After my dad passed away, where was I supposed to go? I would assume the place that I spent 34 hours a week at would provide help. No student should have to pay hundreds of dollars to talk to someone.

As ASB president, I heard every generic concern possible: How can we get test scores up? Getting students more engaged in class? At one point I was given a list of 150 issues and future goals, none of which included the mental and overall health of students despite the crisis we face in society today. And I'm ecstatic to announce I found a solution to many of these generic concerns. No, it's not more studying. It's not more discipline. It's something that cannot be taught or emphasized in calculus class or some standardized test. It's reaching out to the student who struggles with mental illness and has nowhere to go. The student who's having a rough day and needs someone to open up to. The student who's has been struggling financially and has a hard home life. The student who struggles in school but is lost in the system that teaches every student like a cookie cutter. Don't get me wrong: it's not the fault of these underpaid, compassionate, loving adults who work in education ; they work in a broken system that merely looks at students as dollar signs and test scores.

Everyone needs help at some point, but the sad reality is there just hasn't been the resources or awareness. Times are changing. After two years of advocating, hundreds of meetings, and countless committees, I'm beyond excited to announce that a plan is being implemented to bring on a school psychologist at THS. If this issue has been on your heart, I'd love to hear how it has affected you, what this could do for you, and what more I can do. Remember, you are loved! People care about you! Always put yourself first.

Signed,
#Makingachange

September 25, 2018

Am I mad? Am I going crazy? Am I delusional? Those are the questions I asked my psychologist today, and you know what she said? "What do you think?" What do I think? Well, I think I am paying you to tell me if I think I am going crazy. I guess it doesn't work like that. All I know is, I think the thoughts in my head are real. I think my brain is delusional in the sense that everyone around me is lying to me. But how am I supposed to know if my feelings and thoughts are factual or false? I don't know if I will ever truly get an answer.

So this journal entry is for all those who feel like they're going crazy, all those who are stuck in their minds, all those who feel like the world doesn't understand them, because believe me, the feelings are mutual. Have you ever felt like you were the only one on the planet? Have you ever felt like you're different from everyone else? Have you ever felt like your mind, body, and soul are meant for another dimension? Well, I do. I guess it's good to be different, but still, I wish I could relate to someone somehow, you know? Not even my own twin sister I can relate with. My mind feels lost in this so-called sensible world.

"So what do I do?" you are probably asking? Well, I wait and wait and wait, like my mother says, for that good day to come. But, it's been five years, and I am still waiting, so it beats the shit out of me when I don't have to wait anymore.

September 27, 2018

From Hidden Figure,

I felt like a hidden figure today because everything I said, everything I did, every walk I took I felt fake. I didn't want to make it seem as if standing in the Starbucks line bothered me, so I didn't say anything and kept talking to my sister. I didn't want to make it seem as if the voices in my head weren't screaming at me internally while in class, so I said a joke. I didn't want to make it seem as if I am not totally frustrated with my overall appearance while being in the car, so I put the music on and avoided it. I am what you call a hypocrite because everything that comes out my mouth, every action I portray in front of people, is not how I am internally feeling inside.

But, I have one question that I constantly ask myself: Who else is doing the exact same thing as me? Who else is walking around pretending to be someone there not? It just sucks because for a slight moment or hour, I appear normal, my life feels perfect, my body feels sensational. And then I go home and suddenly realize that wasn't me. I go back into my old self of who I truly am, and I hate her. It sucks that I have to be back to my regular, depressed, self-conscious, boring, and annoying self. I wish I felt like that girl I was pretending to be all day. I wish I felt that confident every day. But guess what? I don't. I hate having to pretend. I hate having to fake a smile; it feels worse than not smiling at all. I hate having to fake being happy; it feels worse than being depressed because once I go into my bed at night, or once I am by myself, I know who I truly am.

I just pray to God that I connect to someone who is going through the exact same thing as me. It feels lonely having to pretend who I am, it feels uncomfortable, and it feels discouraging. I metaphorically feel like a mirror. You know, when you look at yourself in the mirror, you see your face but can't actually see what the feelings are inside. I felt like I was wearing a mask or a Halloween costume today, because I wasn't being the person that I am; I was pretending to be someone that is visually and holistically more appealing. It sucks.

On a side note, I don't feel like my psychologist or the pills I am taking are working. I don't feel like anything is working. I am so flustered. I hate that I had to pretend today, but I did it so that I don't seem so ill inside and out.

Signed,
The girl in a mask

September 28, 2018

It's Friday; thank God almighty I survived the week. No school today, and it feels amazing. I feel so blessed to have survived yet another week in this world. And guess what? I am still alive. It just bothers me that I can't have the courage to go out tonight with my cousins because of the way I am feeling and my fear of disappointment. I feel discouraged every time I go out, and I don't want to relive it yet again tonight. Well, the bright side is I got more stories to share with you. In the next pages, these individuals are nothing but inspiring, and if they can overcome obstacles, so can I and so can you.

I have one word for you today: hope. I have hope for all the lonely individuals, I have hope for myself, I have hope for better days, I have hope for everyone going through struggles, and I have hope for a better tomorrow. I decided to create my own acronym for hope, and that is Happier Once People Evolve, because that's really what I want out of the word. I feel better once people start realizing what life really is and who people truly are. It's sad to say, but people don't realize how they treat others. People don't realize that the person you are making fun of or talking bad about can easily set a trigger that can change his or her life forever. Trust me, I know. The last person who made fun of me changed my life for the past five years—and not in a good way. So don't be the last individual to cost someone her life. Don't be the one individual to push someone into going into depression. Don't be the last person to drive someone into locking himself in a basement. It is time for us as humans to evolve into creating better lives for others, not destroy them.

It is crazy how much people affect others. Think about it: you could be that one individual who can change someone from ending her life today with one word, one gesture, or even one acknowledging smile. I know if someone randomly did that to me, I wouldn't feel so down on myself. Also, as much as I hate to admit it, my father is right when he says people need other people to survive in this world. Think about it. There would be no jobs, no school, no parties, no restaurants, no houses, no grocery stores, no weddings, and no nothing without each other. So why is it that we are making fun of the people we need? Why is it we are tearing down their dreams? Why is it we are letting mental illness, addictions, rape, or any other issue people are facing take a back seat?

My challenge for you is whether you are at school, work, the grocery store, a party, the mall, or even the movies, simply acknowledge someone with a smile or even a simple "How are you doing today?" It can change someone's life forever. Remember that I love you and always will.

From @thatoneguymarlito,

30 days of Marlon: A guy who's loving, caring and loyal. A man who loves hard and gives it him all. One that has overcame many obstacles just like everyone else. As everyone knows, September is a special month to me, as it is my birth month. Many know I'm very open and love to tell my truth. Behind the man, there's a boy. A boy who used to

be insecure, teased, picked on, made fun because of his weight and looks. Your typical teenage bullying. Well, that boy, almost 11 years ago in 2007 battled depression that changed his view on life forever. A depression caused by multiple factors including sexual abuse. At a young age, I was sexually assaulted. It made me hate men. It caused a rift between my brothers and myself, an anger towards my dad as I felt like the men who were supposed to protect me and teach me how to fend for myself, didn't. At 16, I would have reoccurring nightmares and in December 2017, I attempted to take my life away. I don't tell my story for pity, nor have I ever tried to victimize myself. I share my past because I reached a point in life where I'm finally ready to close every chapter from my past: experiences, relationships, etc and move forward. You never know the person you least expect, might be battling a demon and eventually that demon becomes so much that they decide to take their own lives. Reach out, talk to someone, Don't Keep quiet. My biggest regret was never speaking up.

Signed, #Letsgetmoving

From @fearlessbipolar,

When you're suffering from any mental health issue, people assume that you may not have the best judgment. Therefore, you aren't always given the credit to make your own decisions. This is especially true when you are manic/hypomanic.

I am definitely happy to give up my decision-making abilities when I am full-blown manic. Full-blown manic can feel like someone else is controlling my body. I've written across bright white cupboards in permanent marker in this state, and I have forgotten my own identity. But then there is hypomania. Hypomania is the lesser form of mania. I still feel the surges of energy and impulsiveness, but I feel significantly more grounded and in control.

One time I was admitted to the hospital while in a full-blown manic episode; it eventually wore off and became a hypomanic episode. They continued to detain me to "make sure I was stable." I had already been there for weeks, and there was really no reason to keep me there. At this time, I called a legal aid, met with a lawyer in my unit, and organized a hearing to earn my discharge. The result? I won. They were wrongly holding me there based on the "likelihood of harming myself or others" (which I have never done, even in full-blown mania). Doing this was in direct violation of my health-care provider's advice.

Although I appreciate the system and understand why it is in place (and it has helped me on many occasions), I want to stress how strongly I feel about taking my health into my own hands. I always respect my psychiatrist's opinion, but doing what makes sense to me is the only way to grow and learn to stand on my own two feet.

Following my heart has been the only thing that
has kept me going on this journey.

Signed,
#Followyourheart

October 2, 2018

As the days get shorter, I don't know how much longer I want
to be here. My thoughts are uncontrollable; my body is physically
incapable of keeping up with school, family, working out, and my
brain. It's exhausting. I feel as though I have no importance or
purpose, as if the only spirits keeping me alive are God and Jesus
following the only human being, my sister. Can anyone hear me?
Does anyone know I exist with a classroom full of students? Does
anyone realize that there is someone in their classroom who is
contemplating life? I feel as if I am a walking illusion. I feel as if I
am not really walking, talking, eating, or breathing right now. I
feel as if someone else has taken over my existence. If only I could
go back to five years ago, when my life was normal. I know God
has a plan for me; I just wish I could walk into it sooner rather
than later. I just wish I could walk his path tonight that leads me
to my happiness, that leads me to all my answers, that leads me
to never having psychological pain.

God, I know you love me, but I need something more. I need
something more than your love and my sister's love to keep me
going through these days that feel unfulfilled. I want to walk
in your plan for me. I want my family to not have to agonize to
watch me like this anymore. I genuinely hope there is something
coming for me soon, because I don't have a reason for why I
should still continue on. The word of today is *anticipation*, because
I don't know what is to come for me. All I know is from the
Serenity Prayer, "We have to accept the things we cannot change,

courage to change the things we can and wisdom to know the difference." It's hard to accept some things in my life right now, but I know that I am walking the path that God has for me, and even though I don't want to believe it, I am exactly where I am supposed to be. I know that the suffering I am going through right now will be worth it once it's all over because it makes me a stronger individual. I know that if God didn't think I could handle it, I wouldn't be going through it. Just remember that God will never give us something we can't do.

October 8, 2018

As I awoke this morning, I discovered a revelation. The question is not "What's wrong with you?" but simply "What has happened to you?" I play the self-blame card daily—that it is my fault, my wrong, my obsessiveness that has brought me here today. But in actuality, it was my perception of the situation that occurred years ago that has brought me to where I am right now. Why is it that I care so much about what people think? Why is it that the voices inside my head are controlling every move I make? Those are the answers I am starting to acknowledge day by day. I know that part of it is fragmented into two parts, which are my personality and society.

There is no denial that society can change your life for better or worse. I am a strong believer that if society wasn't so cruel sometimes or so set in its ways, there would be fewer mental problems. Also, my personality dictates that I love being considered normal and conforming to the stereotypes of what is considered a human being worthy of love, friends, belonging, and everyday existence. I hope I can change my perceptions of the world soon because it is clearly ruining the way I live my life and, I am sure, most of yours too.

From @thesilentkiller,

From a great day yesterday to a struggle day today! Story of my life. It's mostly crap, how this illness can mess your life and plans in an instant and have such control over so many of your thoughts and actions. I need to reiterate: this is a horrible way to live life. Horrible, horrible, horrible! Tried to capture the look on my face while struggling to will myself to get up and out of bed. I really wanted to cry and felt like dying with the amount of effort it took … and that's not exaggerating; that's putting it mildly. Then 12:40 p.m. came, and I was literally forced to get down to sleep because my daughter has a party tonight and needed to get something at the shops …

Needless to say, I am so grateful that I didn't have to drive because that alone would have been another mission impossible for me today. I thank God daily for my small but oh so amazing support structure. These are the days of life with depression—so annoying and flipping irritating, I might add. I'm back home, and guess where I am now? You guessed it: my bed. Need to sleep, please!

#Tiredfordays

From @lacdoodles,

"You don't look ill" is an extremely common and extremely irritating thing many people will hear when they have a mental illness. And often it is said in a very accusatory or disbelieving way. Do I have to prove my illness by looking different? Yes, I have had times where I haven't had the energy to wash or get changed … but just because I'm dressed and looking presentable doesn't mean I have miraculously healed. I luckily don't hear "You look fine" too much anymore, but since I started interacting with people a lot more about their own mental health, I see people criticizing us for not looking "ill enough." It's such bullshit, and it makes me furious. What would you like me to look like? When I had to hand in my notice at my previous job, while I was crying and trying to explain why I had to leave, one of my managers said, "But you've always looked fine." Mental health has no look! Basically, this stupid attitude of people having to look "ill" needs to stop!

#Irritated

Saturday, October 20, 2018

Dear Reader,

I am aware that I haven't written in a while, but it's been a journey, to say the least. More like a roller coaster. I am discovering more and more about myself each and every day as the weather changes and the season changes to fall. My psychologist sessions have been toward being mindfulness, and I am on the fifth day of doing meditation. I will tell you this: doing meditation has relieved some tension in my body, along with making me more aware of not caring about certain situations. Also, you're going to laugh, but I am actually coloring. I started coloring mandalas, which are more like artistic pieces of flowers, or intricate designs. It has relaxed me because I feel just like I was in kindergarten, not caring about anything and taking my mind off of the adult stuff in my life.

Nonetheless, as the days progress, it's much harder to sleep. I don't know why. It's just been very difficult to rest my eyes at night. But I will be so tired that I sleep during the day, which is not very helpful because my days haven't been that productive. I feel now more than ever that I know who I am, what my likes are, and what my dislikes are. I know my favorite movies, my favorite foods, my favorite time of the day to go out, my favorite Starbucks drinks, nearly all of my qualities that I kind of lost along the way while being with Nick.

Unfortunately, by spending so much time alone, I discovered this emptiness that is within me and is still currently not being filled. I feel as though there is something missing. I don't want to be forced to laugh; I don't want to be forced to smile. I want this emptiness to be genuinely filled. It scares me that I am not going to be happy, it scares me that I am going to be alone, it scares me to open up to people because I am reserved and because they don't like me or don't want to hang out with me. So right now, it's like a battle between man and nature, like there is so much conflict and war, until there is a reason to not have to metaphorically pick up my sword anymore. Anyway, that's been the days moving forward, so for all those in similar situations, I am going to continuously say hang on tight, because eventually the ride has to stop.

From Ellie,

I wanted to open up more about mental health and my journey so far. I thought this year was going to be the one for me. I'm 21, graduating and could finally start my life and career. Instead it's been a battle of depression and becoming anorexic. I'll never forget the nights and days of constant crying and starving myself because that's the only thing I thought I could do successfully.

But these moments make us stronger. I go back to these times and think, You've been through so much, you can make it through this meal, and you can make it through this night.

I can say that I'm happy to be here, graduating and showing myself that I am stronger than I thought I was. At points I didn't think I was going to make it. These battles take time and can seem impossible, but they're doable.

Mental illness can change people's behavior in so many different ways. If people you know have changed or become distant, please let them know you're there for them. A simple message to check up on them could save their lives.

Remember that you do have self-worth and that there is help around. It's okay to struggle, but it's also okay to want help to get out of that struggle. The difficulty of remaining strong and positive is half the challenge of recovery and healing, but we will come out the other side.

Signed,
#Healing

Chapter 22

In Between

I call this chapter "In Between" because I am currently straddling the point of what I perceive as being recovered but am not exactly there yet. I can see the finish line as if I was running a marathon, and like all good races, you're in first place. However, did I mention you're in a position where the race is half over? At this point, you've completed half a marathon, so congratulations. But you are not only physically getting tired, you are mentally and emotionally running out of ways to keep going. So what do you do?

This is me right about now. I am in the in-between stage on October 26, 2018. I am not fully ready to go out into the world, but I am working on ways on how to get there. I turned down another evening with my sister and her friends. Go figure. I just don't feel comfortable going to a restaurant full of people and feeling the odd one at the table. I feel as if everyone is judging me, and I feel discouraged to even speak to the people there. I'm sick and tired that at every event I end up going to, my self-esteem weakens, which is why I end up not showing up to places like where my sister is going tonight. I don't want to be disappointed again. I don't want to feel this way when I go out. It's not a feeling that is supposed to show up. You are supposed to have a good time, you are supposed to laugh, and you are supposed to feel comfortable. I just want the clock to rewind to when I had that feeling again. Now I am faced with this burden of hesitation every time I go out because of the events that previously transpired days, weeks, or months ago, when I attempted to go and it was exactly what I expected, a disappointment.

Am I ever going to be the way I was before? I don't exactly know. But until I feel comfortable with the uncomfortable, I guess I will be stuck in the in-between stage for a while. A shout-out to all those people feeling this way now, or who have previously felt this way. I just can't seem to get out of the house. It's my safety net, and I feel comfort in knowing that life can't harm me from in here. I feel security knowing that I won't be ridiculed or made fun of, I won't feel uncomfortable or disrespected, because I have safe things: my family, my TV, my phone, and not a soul to disappoint me.

However, there is just one problem: the only relationship I have created in my house is with my couch. Is there anyone who understands? Am I ever going to have a positive experience when I go out? And am I ever going to metaphorically get to the finish line? These are the questions I am asking myself. I guess you have to read on to find out the answers, and I guess I have to live a bit more to find out for myself.

From Abigail,

I never thought I'd be the person to dedicate my time and awareness to anything like this, but before my sister, I was so clueless to suicide awareness. I never considered that people could be struggling so much but never showed that they were. It was obvious that my sister was struggling, but I never thought we'd lose her in such a way that we did. Every day I remember you, Lily Vac, and every day I miss you so much. There are so many things that I wish I could say to you again. So many times I wish I could hug your body. I will always remember the funny, goofy girl that you were. The one who embarrassed me in public, the one who pushed me so far out of my comfort zone. The one who blasted silly songs like "Bodak Yellow" by Cardi B and knew every word to it, or any song for that matter. You are so precious, you are so loved, you are so beautiful, and you are greatly missed.

Signed,
#EveryDayIRememberYou

October 31, 2018

Stories like the ones above remind me constantly that there are people suffering in this world, and their battles might just be greater than mine. Today is Halloween, and for the first time today, I get to pretend to be someone I'm not for a change. I get to put on a costume and a mask that is not even close to who I am. It feels incredible to be someone else for a change. I hate to admit it, but every day I am finding more and more things that set me apart from the rest of my family and the world. It's okay, I tell myself, because I know that I am different. Anyway, I am blessed for this day because I am able to have the freedom to be anyone I want today I can be a celebrity who is rich, I can be the next bachelorette, I can be a nurse or a doctor, I can be anything imaginable for the day. For the first time, I feel infinite due to the endless possibilities to be someone other than my lonely, scared, fearful, depressed self. I get to make myself feel powerful—until the clock strikes midnight that is.

Regardless, this is a reminder to all those who want to be someone else that you can do so today. I encourage all those to pick who they aspire to be like or look like, and then be it today. Honestly, if you want to feel sexy, then do it; if you want to be scary, do it. It's the one day of the year that you get to be the person behind the mask. Also, for all those contemplating your life, you can actually feel dead today—not that I'm encouraging you do so. But you can dress up as a mummy, the walking dead, or even a ghost and for the first time be hidden from the world.

I have decided that my costume this year is being the woman I was prior to being diagnosed with anxiety and depression. I have decided to dress up very fancy, put on my makeup, and go to school as if I wasn't mentally unstable. I am actually looking forward to today; all my worries and fears are going to be thrown out the window because I can be anyone I want for the day. As I take my old self out into the world today and mask all of my emotions. I wonder how the people around me are going to react. After all, it is Halloween.

Saturday, November 3, 2018

"The journey of a thousand miles begins with one step," said Lao Tzu. I realized today that I haven't taken that first step yet. You're probably confused right about now because the whole book thus far has been talking about my first steps to wellness, and I devoted a whole chapter on the first step. However, in order to walk the path of wellness and not be scared, it takes that first step, which I have not done yet. I can't seem to get out of the four walls I am always talking about. I am still in this basement, and if you're wondering whether Halloween went well, it didn't. I got my sister dressed and stayed home eating cereal. So no, I didn't take that first step to the unknown yet. I am so scared of how people are going to treat me. I am so scared that I am not good enough. I am so scared that the guy I like won't like me because he will find all the flaws I hate in myself. That's the first step I am talking about, and I am sure all of you can relate.

We are scared to take the first step to either marriage, a house, getting pregnant, a first date, and more. You have been avoiding that step, so you do everything in your power to do anything but that. I encourage you to do so because maybe if I see someone else taking a first step, I won't be so scared.

I am aware there is a life that lies ahead of me aside from the safety of my home. But until I actually witness it, I am still not taking that first step right now. I am still in the stage of not forgiving those who have done me wrong, not forgiving myself, not letting go of the past, and being doubtful of my future endeavors. I'm sorry, first step, but you're going to have to wait a little longer for me.

Signed,
#scared

From @ Jasminesarayoga,

In the past week, I have had sleep paralysis and a panic attack, unconsciously picked the skin around my fingers to pieces out of anxiety, sobbed my heart out, and snapped at family out of overwhelm. In the past week, I have also laughed my head off, listened attentively to others, been kind, done a good job in front of housework, taught carefully, put together a yoga class, hugged my family and told them I love them, and looked after myself well. Being human is a rich tapestry of different emotions and experiences. During my meditation, I represent a place of calm within that is always there even if sometimes it feels less accessible than at other times. I ride the breath to come here. In my yoga study trip to India, there was ups and downs too, but ever present was this place of calm deep within.

Why am I writing this? Because sometimes we can't help but compare on social media and feel like other people are somehow doing this being human thing "better." Sometimes we see the highlights reel and tell ourselves we are the only ones struggle. That's not true. People have their own difficulties to work with and their own joys too. This is why I came to yoga: to help me deal with and manage my own personal set of challenges, and to appreciate in full the vast range of human experience. Namaste. Sending loving to anyone reading this.

Signed,
#Healingthesoul

From @psychedforstrength,

I have depression. I've been a victim to suicidal ideation. I've come close to ending my life multiple times. My heart races as I admit this for others to read. But I've come to realize there is no shame in feeling suicidal. It's okay to be depressed. For those struggling, you are not weak for thinking these thoughts. You're strong, and you've felt like you've been fighting for so long. You are strong, so keep fighting. It can get better. It does get better. I'm proud that you're alive.

From @mattxsantos,

The year 2018 has mentally been one of the toughest for me to deal with since I've been back home. From working every day of the week to losing friends, love, and family to trying to accept myself for who I am, it's all been an uphill struggle. Sometimes beautiful things arise from disasters—catalysts that are so profound, you struggle to understand them, but they change your whole perception of what living truly is. I've been blessed to receive this change of mind state and lifestyle, this new way of thinking to be the best me, and it feels fucking good.

Signed,
#AcceptingMyself

From @faithfully_led,

As men, we often aren't looked at as having feelings, and we have to be strong in the face of adversity. Oftentimes the adversity is something we have never planned for, and we get kicked in the gut, pushed down, and made to feel like we are worthless. I was told this by several people after my divorce and during the time leading up to it. As men, we can handle most things, and we can even compartmentalize things, but they hurt just as much as if we showed it. Think about what you say next time, because men are human too, hurt just as the next person—and they may not be able to process these words in a way that could be healthy. Men are three times more likely to commit suicide due to something traumatic as divorce or separation. Words matter, and words break bones and spirits.

Signed,
#WordsHurt

Monday, November 19, 2018.

You're probably wondering how I have been feeling lately because I haven't written in a while. Well, I can tell you this: not so good. I am still in this constant state of thinking there is something wrong with me and thinking that everyone is judging me. What do I do? Is it possible to just be normal? Is it possible that I can be normal for one fucking day? If you haven't guessed it, words do hurt. I am constantly stuck in the past and thinking about all of the horrible words that people have said to me over the years. I wonder whether I will ever get over it. Do you ever wonder whether you could go back in time and change some things? Well, I wish I could. I wish I could change something that triggered my depression to exist for the last five years. I wish I could go back in time and change what triggered my anxiety, or my state of being, or my suicidal thoughts. If only I had a time machine. I think life would be easier if you knew what was going to happen in the future so that you can do everything in your power to stop all of the negative things from occurring.

Signed,
If only I could turn back time

From @ jesshutchensfit,

Finally, at my happiest, but getting here was not easy. My freshmen year of college, at just 19 years old, I discovered my father was having an affair with a girl my age. He left my mom (married 22 years) and 5 little brothers for this girl to start their own family. How did I handle this? By drinking heavily and binge eating. I gained 50 pounds and self-sabotaged for a year straight.

When I was 25, just 8 months before my wedding and after years of working on my relationship with my father, he committed suicide because this same girl cheated on him. This was awful and so hard. But this time around, I put my trust in God and continued on with the gym. I left my teaching job because I realized life was too short. I did not self-sabotage …

If you're going through something awful, just know you're not alone. We all have struggles, and I'm here to tell you life will get better! Give it time, but I promise you can find happiness and truly love yourself and your life.

Signed,
#Finally

From @Miss Mimi Elizabeth,

Imagine having so much anxiety that your body is filled with so much pain that moving is almost impossible. Imagine that your thoughts don't slow down no matter how many pills you take, and they tell you to do all kinds of things you know aren't rational but you can't ignore. So instead of dealing with all the pain, you never leave the house because when you do, you can't step on the cracks in the sidewalks or else something bad might happen.

The depression is really more than an intense feeling of wanting to die every minute of the day.

Even when I'm smiling, the feeling is still there, and it has been since I can remember. It washes over me and makes me feel like I can't even talk or move my body, and eating becomes something I need to force myself to do. Nothing is enjoyable. Everything causes intense pain to me. Then I take one medication on top of another, and those cause me to have no energy on top of the little I have to begin with, or more anxiety, or a mouth so dry that I feel like no amount of water can remedy the situation. The headaches, the weight gain, the uncontrollable muscle movements, and every single side effect I have ever gotten from these medications would be worth it if they made me feel better. But I have taken them for over a decade, mostly in batches of five or more, and still the darkness looms over me. Still the thoughts plague me. The compulsions. The physical pain. All my symptoms still there on top of all the side effects. So I don't leave the house. I can't work. I can't go to school. I have had to accept that I am disabled and might have to suffer my entire life this way. The fifteen years I dedicated to therapy, exercise (and becoming a Pilates teacher), and doing everything I could to help myself provided little relief at times. But looking back on my notes and my behaviors, still all there was is suffering.

I cannot suffer any longer. I really have just been living for my family so that I don't hurt them if I decide not to live. But I can't begin to explain my suffering in writing because I'm not a good writer. I hope one day people understand people like me and can come up with better treatment.

Signed,
#Don't want to suffer

December 24, 2018

It's Christmas Eve, and before I get to how things are going with me, I just want to mention that I had the pleasure of texting Mimi Elizabeth, and let me tell you, she's scared. I told her that I am scared as well, but you just have to keep the faith because I am actually starting to heal. Today, I am proud to say that I am at least 60 percent better, which statistically is good because it means I'm more than halfway to being 100 percent, or at least 99 percent because it's rare that there is a person who feels perfect. Nevertheless, I am stronger and wiser today than I have been in years with the help of my psychologist and, yes, my medication.

You're probably wondering how it is possible she recovered so quickly. I will name you three of my secrets: exercise, mediation, and family. Exercise has helped me to get rid of my internal and external insecurities that I have been battling with for quite a while now. Even though they're not all gone, they have reduced due to sweating away all of my worries. Meditation has helped me be in the present moment, and let me tell you, if you're not being present, you should start. Trust me, you will feel so lucky to be alive in each moment that you endure and are grateful for each day.

Lastly, my family. They have been my biggest support system. My mom and dad have challenged me in ways I couldn't have imagined. My sister, also known as my best friend, has been so patient and understanding every single day of this journey. But, above all, it's my Nonna because of the endless love she provides to our entire family. Her generosity inspires me to become just like her when I am her age. I have decided to take each day as God intended it and to not worry about what people are saying about me. If you were truly a decent human being, you wouldn't judge me— and if you do judge me, then I don't need you in my life. So, yes, I am proud to say I am getting better. The one thing this journey (which is soon to end) has taught me is that life is easy and that all good things are coming my way.

Signed,
#Love is in the air

From @michellewalton_detroit,

It's okay to not be okay … Read these words and believe them with every part of your soul, because these words have the power to change your life.

Like so many, I too struggle with mental health. Some days I wake up and feel like I can conquer the world. Other days, it's a struggle to just put on pants. I've tried pretty much every method and medication out there aimed to make me "normal," whatever that even means. But the biggest, most important tool I have adopted is the belief that it's okay to not be okay …

Accepting ourselves for who we are and allowing ourselves to truly feel all the things (good or bad) is the most freeing thing we can do for ourselves. Why? Because, we are human … I am human. You are human. Our babies, our spouses, our family, and our friends—we are all human! And that whole "being human" thing means that sometimes we might not be the perfect version of ourselves. But you know what? That is okay!

Once we learn to accept how we feel and who we are, we can encourage others to love and accept us the way we deserve. So from now until the end of time, I challenge you to be okay with not being okay. Okay? Wishing everyone a positive, happy, and healthy life.

Signed,
#Truth

January 26, 2019

It is currently twenty-six days into the new year. I am almost at 80 percent recovered, and I feel amazing. There is just one problem: there are still other people in this world who have not yet recovered or who have given up trying. Yesterday, it saddens me to hear that an individual in my life has died from a drug overdose. Despite the #bellletstalk and other campaigns, why is it that the death rate due to mental health keeps rising? Please, if you know anyone—whether it is a friend, an acquaintance, or a family member—do whoever you have to and get them help. It is a serious matter that truly devastated a family I am close with to know that their son, nephew, cousin, and grandson has died due to something that wasn't given more awareness. I hope I can start a march, a fund, or a charity one day, along with the publishing of this book, because I can't hear about another person having suffered from a drug overdose, a suicide attempt, a mental health disorder, or whatever the case may be that could be prevented. These people deserve to be living.

Signed,
#Let'sgethelp

From @faithmorgan,

The first time I planned on killing myself, I was 15 years old. I was determined, and no one was going to stop me. But after finding myself in a hospital bed, the next 8 days were a blur of sleep and sickness and nothing more.

The second time, there was no note; there was no plan. Instead, I impulsively grabbed a bottle of pills and began shoving them down my throat, thinking this would be my last breath on this beautiful earth.

That attempt may have been my last, but I'd be lying if I said I never considered trying again. The good news is I've been able to keep those dark thoughts at bay. With therapy and medication, I am able to manage both my depression and anxiety. I was also lucky enough to survive my two previous attempts, after which I sat up. I walked away—forever changed, but alive.

And I am not alone. We don't talk about suicide because of shame, secrecy, or fear. We don't talk about suicide because of the stigma. Our silence has produced many myths, stereotypes, and "crazy" that we see on TV. I hope one day to change that. I hope to inspire and help others with my story. I hope by this point I can inspire just one person. Or just help one person to reach out and get help. I am determined to get rid of the nasty stigma that goes along with mental health. You are not alone. You are not crazy. You are not dramatic. You are not selfish.

You are loved. You are worthy. You are worth it. You are needed.

Be patient in the pain.

Signed,
#Iwalkedaway

February 2, 2019

A wise man by the name of Steve jobs once said,

You can't connect the dots looking forward; you can only connect them looking backwards. So you have to trust that the dots will somehow connect in your future. You have to trust in something—your gut, destiny, life, karma, whatever. This approach has never let me down, and it has made all the difference in my life.

Personally, I don't care whether or not you believe in his words. All I care is that you read them and understood the meaning behind the profound message. Think about it: How many times in your life have you doubted your school major, your current profession, or your commute to work? It's because you are not tremendously passionate about what you are doing.

Now, this is where all of you say, "But it brings me money, which allows me to buy what I love." However, you are not seeing the true essence behind the things you love. If you don't love what you do, why are you doing it? Trust me, money comes. Look how long it takes doctors or lawyers to make money, at least seven years. Believe me, everything in life will come once you find what you are passionate about.

So how does this relate to mental health? Well, if you stop thinking about your anxiety, depression, suicidal thoughts, and any other mental illness for a second, and if you think about what you love doing, it can suddenly change your life toward recovery. For me, I love writing. I am passionate about love, hate, religion, law, working out, or whatever the topic may be. Once I became diagnosed with depression and anxiety, I started writing journals, stories, letters to God, you name it. I felt an instant gratification of relief knowing I told someone, even if it was just my piece of paper. This was my step to my recovery because whether it was fifteen minutes, thirty minutes, one hour, or longer that I was writing, it made me forget about being stuck and thinking about how sad I felt, knowing that no one feels my struggle. Since then, I woke up one day and said, "I am going to write a book so that whether the person reads one page or every page, I know that the dots connected them to read those words."

I want you to remember the road of recovery lies within, which means it starts with taking the action of pursuing what you're good at. Even if you don't believe in God, you were created on this earth to do something, so find that one thing. Think about all the people in your life; they provide you with that one thing that they were meant to do, and the dots connected them despite all their trials and tribulations. Trust this process; it will lead you to share your story, it will lead you to your profession, and it will lead you to recovery. For instance, if you're passionate about recovering from your current state, do everything in power to do so, and the dots will eventually lead you to finding your true happiness. Almost 99 percent of the people on this earth don't know how they do what they do because it is based on intuition; they were called to what they are currently doing. If you don't believe me, ask around. I assure you that their profession eventually chose them because they have a motivation to do what they are doing. In my life, my mom was destined to be a hairdresser because she was never good at math, science, or writing, but she was creative with drawing, which led her to a profession that allowed her to use her hands. You see, regardless of the situation you are in right now, you can change it by doing something you love. If you love drawing, working out, reading, and playing music, do these every day, whether it is in between school, work, eating, meeting up with friends, being in rehab, or being in the hospital. After all, it's not about money, power, materialistic desires—it is about being you. Overall, we can all agree that is the best gift that you will ever come across.

Chapter 23

A Star Is Born

February 8, 2019

Ayn Rand once said, "The question isn't who is going to let me; it's who is going to stop me."

For the first time in a long time, I woke up today and said, "Fuck it. I am done being sick." I decided to play some music, dance around my bedroom, and start praising God for keeping me alive. However, it wasn't until the music stopped when it suddenly dawned on me that if I want to change my mental health state, it is going to start with my attitude toward life. Today, I decided to appreciate everything around me, and it became clear that there is nothing I should be complaining about. I am healthy, I am beautiful, I am smart, I am a wonderful spirit, and I am a good person.

Most of you at this point are probably saying to yourself, "We have heard this about you before in your previous chapters." But, guess what? I actually saw myself in the mirror today and believed every single word for the first time—and it felt fucking amazing. I haven't never felt this way in such a long time, and nobody is going to stop me from feeling this way for the rest of my life. No one is going to take away any goal of mine, no one is going to stop me from falling in love, and no one is going to stop me from being happy. It took a long time for me to feel this way, and I am not letting anyone take that away from me.

This is why I am writing to all of you today: because your day is coming. For me, even though it took five years to get where I am today, and even though I am not 100 percent, at least I've gotten here. Please don't give up; your time is on the horizon. I love you, and you are worth feeling what I am feeling today. I promise that you will; simply give it time. As I mentioned before, there is a time for everything, and your time may not be today, but you will know it, and you are going to thank the ground that you walk on that you didn't give up because this feeling today is absolutely speechless. I did it, and I can't wait to see how the rest of my life falls into place now.

Sadly there is not enough pages in the world to write down my whole life story. However, I promise not to end it here because I can't wait to tell you the moment that I have fallen truly in love, the moment I have graduated from university, and other great moments that I am sure will be entertaining to read. I believe in my heart all good things are coming. As for you, trust me that all good things are coming because after all, life is good, life is easy, and all good things are on their way.

February 14, 2019

Today inspired me to write not only because it's one of my favorite holidays but because it's this day full of love that pushed me to writing in the first place. Specifically, it's the love of something that every living human can relate to: life.

If I Stay …
If I stay,
I won't miss out on a greater day.
If I stay,
I will not miss out for the wait of the rainbow on
that rainy day.

110

If I stay,
I will get to hear my sister say she loves me in
every which way.
If I stay,
Every step I take will be a reminder of how strong
I'm becoming, throughout every hour of the day.
If I stay,
God will grant me more perfect ways to be his
forever angel, with a halo ray.
If I stay,
Falling in love will just have a reason to cross my
pathway.
If I stay,
I won't regret another day on the fourth of May
(my birthday).
If I stay,
My current life won't seem like a dreadful push
of a snow sleigh.
If I stay,
I promise not to hold on to yet another cliché.
If I stay,
Maybe the world won't seem so gray.
If I stay,
I will make sure that every room I walk into, I
slay.

Thank you, God, for allowing me not to hurt in dismay.
I choose today to not even question the words,
If I stay …

February 21, 2019

I discovered a great theory today—the theory of success. I am sure all of you have been told if you look the other way, you may miss out on what is right in front of you. I am reaffirming this profound message because I realized it is the key to life. It is the key that opens every door, it is the key that opens every treasure chest, and it is the key that opens the portal to recovery. Think about it: every great basketball player shot a three-pointer based on being present in the game and not looking to the sidelines at the fans. Also, every great hockey player skated to the net to shoot the puck at the last few minutes of the third period because he was focused in the moment. In relation to real life, the best cops caught their criminals by not taking their eyes off the crime scene.

Regardless of how you interpret it, if you look away, walk away, or think about something else other than the moment you are in, you are going to miss out on your metaphorical three-pointer or the winning goal. This is where success lies: it lies in where you are right now and being aware of what you are doing every second of the day. Trust me, life passed me by for a while until I realized that I was waking up all wrong. I missed out on life's greatest moments because I was stuck in my head, didn't get out of bed, didn't pay attention, or decided to look away for even a minute. This is why I want you to start realizing the next time you are with people, or in a room, or at a job interview, or at a family or friend event, you should be fully present. It is the solution to solving all of your problems. I don't want you missing out on anything just because you think you are stuck, or you think you are not worthy to be in a room, or you go somewhere and are not having a good time. In actuality, you create your moments, and before you know it, you're going to be eighty years old and regretting that you didn't see so many of the amazing things that life put in front of you. Your time is now, and guess what? It always has been. You simply didn't have the eyes to notice it. Thank you, God, for allowing me to finally see through mine.

April 13, 2019

Dear Reader,

If you are at this point, this means that you have discovered something about me that I have just experienced. I was driving on the road around midnight, the air clear and slightly cold. I didn't have the radio on because for the first time, I wanted to drive in silence so that I could escape the loudness of this world. All of sudden, I drove faster than normal—so fast that I urged myself to turn the car into a ditch. I could feel my heart coming out of my chest, my airbag almost suffocating me until I couldn't breathe. Then the car stopped. I sat in the car seat, frozen, and I could hear the sirens from the fire trucks and ambulance around the corner, knowing it was for me. I get up covered with blood from my head scars all the way to my arms, and I noticed that I couldn't feel my body from the waist down. All I could think about in the moment was not "Why did I do it?" but "Thank gosh, because for once in my life, other people whom I don't know will ask me questions about how I am feeling and if they can stay by my side until I get better." The only thing is, I woke up.

I've always loved dreams because they can bring you to a place that your ideal self is unconsciously seeking, and you are able to experience another dimension of the world without people knowing it exists unless you tell them. For me, this dream in particular felt real from the minute it started because I was hoping it would actually happen. I thought to myself that maybe if I did this, a part of me wouldn't keep looking at the past. Yes, I am better, but there are days when I wish I hadn't existed, such as this one, because maybe I would feel better about not dreading another disappointment in life. I know there are good dreams that in reality do come true. However, I wish they would come sooner so that I don't have to be wishing upon another nightmare.

April 19, 2019

You know those stories from social media that I have been reaching out to? Well, guess what? I've got more for you. In particular, one of the stories that touched me emotionally was by a gentleman named Josh Campbell, known as @healthhunk, who doesn't let his mental health define him as he gives back to others through online self-help coaching.

From @healthhunk,

"Feelings are GAY"
Until you're someone like me, bursting at the seams, bottled up and ready to blow. Does that make me gay? Conditioned by the stiff-lipped

sports team and alpha-male Environments-I was confused and numb to the fact self-expression was really the cure to my cancer.

Growing up, popular was to be jack-the-lad-the guy of the moment. To be the laughing stock, leap the bridge first, or call the captain of a team. Throwing out uncool emotion was never a part of this. This was all makeup for coping.

The footy (soccer) scores, girl-talk, and who received "man of the match" beat getting flowery with feelings amongst your pals. Quickly excused as being a "pussy" or thrown under the bus by banter or a swift subject change to the footy (soccer). If only I'd known that your anything and everything in any given moment. To be comprehensive. It's ok to dip in and out of the attributes.

It's human balance which should not be defined by the boxes society creates in gender. To be truly special-be the best of both worlds.

Strong and vulnerable

Funny and grounded

Intellectual and relatable

I'm sure you can think of more …

Let your emotions guide you but not imprison you to compulsive behavior.

It's dangerous, even deadly. Causes suicide, dysfunctional relationships, and personality disorders.

A life without judgment, would be so much better.

Don't you think?

From @mrsclairedeane,

I'm angry that I've slipped again. I'm angry that I need a good cry every couple of days. I'm angry that I need therapy, and I'm angry that I may never have any answers. Inside feels like one big, hot mess right now, but I'm feeling it. I'm doing what I can, and I'm waiting for the anger to subside and make way for peace, make way for love, and make way for kindness. I'm sure it's there in spades. I dole it out all day every day, both in work and at home; it's just myself with whom I neglect to practice.

My friend and I were having one of our weekly "delving deep in the shit" conversations last week, and she said to me, "But why do you question it so hard? It's been a tough year. You've lost and lost again. It was out of your control." She's right: grief is all-consuming. The what-ifs and whys flare up an invisible rage that has no choice but to bubble over, and suddenly it's like a silent agony pact that you get to just carry around. And here I am again with a different kind of grief, losing one of the greatest loves of my life daily to dementia. It's weighting heavily. I know that's life, it's hard, and yada yada, but there's only so much before slowly you break, like a glass pane shattering in slow motion, portraying a calm exterior. But inside, I'm desperately trying to grasp at the pieces to pull them back in, to put them back together, to put myself back together. I could give up, of course, except I don't want to, because although it feels like one big losing streak at times, there are so many wins along the way too. Life's not a fairytale, and I get that, but maybe I need to stop trying to put it all back together. Maybe I need to just breathe and let it all go, let myself crumble, and let my tears fall because I'm not the same anymore. The thing is, I can still lose myself to belly laughs, and I can still feel love and hope in the deepest parts of me, seeping through all the cracks. Maybe that's a win. I'm taking it and running with it.

Every day, I'm taking one step and one breath at a time, feeling every inch of the good and the bad. It's real and it's raw, but you know, that's life, and maybe with that kind of acceptance, that's the only kind of happy ending I'll need.

From @stephbonyoutube,

Forgiveness.

I recently read a post from @iisuperwomenii about not forgiving others, but forgiving yourself. This is something I'm really bad at.

I treat myself like shit. I'm a perfectionist by nature in all areas of my life. I mess up and hurt someone's feelings. That's it—I'm a horrible person. I can't attend something? I need to try harder. I have a really bad mental health day like today! I'm never going to be good enough for anyone because I'm such a downer.

I find it weird how we ourselves are someone we live with day in and day out, yet we find it so hard to give ourselves forgiveness and patience and understanding.

I'm going to be honest. I am super, hyper focused on other people's interactions on this site to the point that if I don't get an emoji back or all these silly things, I go into an overdrive of thinking I'm never enough or not liked as much. These are such unhealthy thoughts. But I attack myself for it like it's my fault. It's like I have to be this perfect person and make everyone like me and make everyone happy. But guess what? That's impossible!

Perfectionism is such a real thing in today's society. So I ask you, like I'm asking myself, to forgive yourself.

Steph, you are doing the best you can. Give yourself grace when you can't do everything and can't accomplish every goal at once. Be okay with not being everyone's favorite. Give yourself grace when the search for who you are isn't always easy. There's so much more I can say. Just be patient.

I often get so afraid to share these things, but I've really found my place in sharing more about mental health. It might not make me the most popular, and it might not always be positive, but when have I ever been that?

If I can help one person feel not alone, then that's worth it.

@camillaelysia,

If you have followed me for a while, then you will know I love to talk about mental health, especially my own, and I have had so much love as a response with people telling me how strong I am. I guess because I only speak about it when I am feeling good again, what you don't see is that to be strong and come through the other side, I have to go through the part that makes me feel weak and worthless. The endless crying and self-hate, my mind paralyzing my body, and not leaving the house for days or getting dressed. I'm going through new therapy at the moment, and I love it for the first time in my life, but it was tough, and it's been taking a toll on me. I wanted to share this with you because you can be strong and still suffer, you can feel great most of the time and still have really bad days, and just because you haven't been diagnosed with something, that doesn't mean the way you feel isn't valid.

People are obsessed with labels, and I actually found being diagnosed with bipolar more damaging than helpful in the long term. Have you ever looked in the mirror and wished you saw something else? Have you ever hurt yourself or thought negative things about yourself? Have you ever blown up at someone for no reason? Have you ever cried yourself to sleep? Have you ever wanted to stay in bed forever with the curtains closed when it's sunny outside? Mental health presents itself in many different forms. You can feel depression and not be clinically depressed. You can feel anxious and not need daily anxiety medication. If you are human, then you have mental health. Physically, we can only understand our own pain, but we can be compassionate about others. Be kind, be supportive, and be attentive to others when you feel you can, but always take care of yourself first, because we are all struggling in some way.

June 10, 2019

Dear Readers,

You know in tug-of-war, when you have two people on each end of the rope desperately trying to make the other person fall by tugging and tugging? Well, this is what I have been doing with my life until today. Looking back on past experiences, I have been playing tug-of-war with the majority of the events that I have come across in my life by complaining about them or by being frustrated in the moments.

Now, think about yourself for a moment. How many times have you resisted a situation, whether it was waiting in a long line, going to a family member's house you didn't like, or complaining at work? I bet you are reading this and saying to yourself, "Countless times." However, by resisting the situation you were put into, it only makes you feel worse, and it creates a reciprocated negative inner energy.

Instead, I want you all to try to smile, laugh, or even say thanks out loud the next time you are in a situation that you don't like. Personally, I can tell you your internal energy of your body changes to having a positive experience in the worst situations. Think about it: would you want the last thing you remember before you die to be the feeling of misery over such a harmless experience? I know I wouldn't. You see, anything can happen in a blink of an eye, and it's so sad that people don't realize that we really do have only one chance at survival. Whether you are three years old or ninety-three years old, the next morning is never a guarantee that you are going be alive. This is the unfortunate reality that I want you to put in perspective: whether or not you are dealing with mental health, because the moment you die, you are unable to say "I love you" to your loved ones again, or eat your favorite food, or drink water. This is the reality of life, and for the first time, I did not resist going to work because I thought about my actual existence and that if I were to die in this moment by sudden chance, I would have wanted to be happier with my time on earth.

I encourage you to make the change of living your life without resisting, because I assure you when you are no longer able to exist, you will regret those times you resisted. Also, ask yourselves if you think God created you to complain about your time that he has given you on earth. I don't think so. God wants you to embrace each moment as it comes because when you are in heaven and get the chance to have that conversation with him, you are going to regret the words "I loved the life you have given me, but I wish I had lived it differently." Most important, to those who are already living their lives in complete happiness and Zen, I encourage you to keep living it, and I hope to graciously cross paths with you one day.

P.S., You don't have to contemplate whether you would have lived your life differently if you make the choice now to start living the life that will make you say, "I love my life, and I would not change a single thing about my time spent here."

June 18, 2019

It's 3:10 p.m., and I am about to walk on my graduation stage after four years. I am hot as hell, to say the least, and will anticipate that I will be like this for another three hours until every single name is called to receive a diploma. You can imagine my excitement at having to sit with over seven hundred students in a room that is warm with little room to breathe. As I sit there, I become insecure because I feel like I am the only person who is struggling with issues, and I become angry that I have to go through yet another situation where I feel horrible about myself. Yet I still try to hide my insecurity by making jokes and laughing with other people.

It is now twelve hours later, 3:00 a.m., and of course I did not sleep, but aside from that, it was weird because at this exact time, I started reminiscing about my high school graduation and how I got to enjoy every single moment due to the fact that I didn't have anything wrong with me. I was able to sit through the entire ceremony and dinner afterward with my parents and have no worries or judgments whatsoever. Flash forward five years, on a similar stage, and I'm feeling the complete opposite, as if my previous life never even occurred. I wish God or someone could have told me what my life would be like after high school so that I could have prevented years of therapists, depression pills, visits to the doctor, and more. I am starstruck because life before my eyes can change, and who knows? Maybe this experience has taught me to wake up and smell the flowers. I should wake up and notice that life does not revolve around me. I should wake up and look at the other billions of other people in this world. That is exactly what I did today.

Today happened to be a blessing in disguise because I felt compassion for others being imperfect. I felt beautiful knowing that I have flaws just like everyone else on that stage. I hadn't even contemplated that five years prior. I graduated, and I finally made it. Thanks, York University. It's been a slice.

June 23, 2019

Dear Readers,

Today I realized something that seems so obvious yet is not obvious to most people. Today, I saw a woman who was anorexic to the point that I am pretty sure I saw her bones through her T-shirt, and she was desperately walking to stay alive. However, the point was not about the anorexic girl; it was that we all have that one thing we wish to change about ourselves, whether it is our weight, our eyes, our blemishes on our face, our nose, our lips, our boobs, our height, or our butt. The list can go on and on. For me, I rather keep what I would like to change private. However, I wish I could desperately change this one thing due to the fact that society has thoroughly convinced me that I am not suitable to be in relationship or meet social standards because of it.

This is when it dawned on me that I am the way I am today mentally because of society's so-called acceptable human laws. I say, Wake the fuck up with this ideal image of the perfect human because it does not exist. Trust me, I am guilty of it all the time. If I look at someone who's dressed differently, I am quick to comment. But today I realized that it's their bodies and their lives, so why should I be the one to ruin it? Why should I be the one to comment something negative about them? I don't know them, so I shouldn't cause them to feel horrible about themselves. That is why I am telling all of you to please not make fun of or talk bad about someone, because believe me, if people could change that one thing that we are all talking about, they would within a millisecond. Unfortunately, life doesn't work that way because there are some things that are unchangeable. But if we embrace and accept not only ourselves but others, we will have fewer people in mental institutions or at home depressed.

For today's life lesson, wash your face with cold water and start seeing and embracing life's imperfections.

June 26, 2019

Dear Readers,

True or false: "All is fair in love and war."

If your answer is true, then you are 100 percent right. But, if your answer is false, then you are also right. You see, this statement is all based on primary beliefs and feelings about love and conflict. Some say that it's true because the only two areas in which you can be forgiven is love and war due to love being unconditional. On the other hand, some people may argue that it's a bunch of bullshit due to the fact that they have probably never felt true, unconditional love. Why am I giving you this philosophical lesson? Well, as hard as it is to believe, I haven't found my soul mate yet, and I am guilty of being a little promiscuous. Nevertheless, I am still in search of my own love and war.

I wanted to address this because as I indicated prior, I assured you that my book will end with some kind of love story. As it turns out, we are getting near the end, and the clock is reaching midnight in fairy tale terms. Don't get me wrong: I love being by myself on this journey of fulfilling my physical, intellectual, and spiritual self. It's just that I know there is a part of me that is missing that one piece of completing the metaphorical Alessia Davi puzzle. For others, it's easy to find that special someone, but for those who are still looking and feeling sorry for yourselves, know that you are not alone. That is why I chose to come to terms with the fact that love really is patient. It is hard for humans like my twin sister and I, who have been emitting love their whole lives and searching for that love in return. By the way, the people who say, "Who cares if you're single?" have either just been in a relationship, are in one, or enjoy being with multiple people at once. So shout-out to those who are still waiting.

My advice is love yourself mentally, trust God, open your heart and soul, and be fully present with life. After all, as the saying goes, love is like the wind: you can't see it, but you can feel it—and this feeling is indescribable.

July 12, 2019

Dear Readers,

On my journey of self-discovery, I am now officially seeing a spiritual healer. What is a spiritual healer? Well, it is someone who is able to heal your whole body, mind, and soul through their words, practices, and spiritual touches. My sessions so far have been uplifting because I have been practicing positive affirmations that I encourage you all to say to yourself every day: you are kind, you are beautiful, you are worthy, and you are powerful.

I also wanted to share with you a little Hawaiian mantra that I have been saying to myself, called the Ho'ponono Pono prayer. Specifically, *Ho'o* means to make it, and *Pono* means right.

Practicing it allows you to be right with yourself and others. The first line of the prayer is, "I am sorry," which allows you to let go of all the times your body has been shamed. The second line of the prayer is "please forgive me," and as you say this, take a moment to notice the responses of your body as you allow forgiveness to resonate within. The third line of the prayer is, "I love you," so allow yourself to feel this unconditional love for your whole self. Finally, the last line is saying "thank you" to every organ and muscle in the body that allows you to move, eat, sleep, and feel pleasure. Trust me: as you ritually say this prayer, every blame, guilt, and regret will suddenly be released. You will unexpectedly feel a sense of compassion and forgiveness throughout your body, and you will be cleansed from any negative thoughts about yourself. However, you must take a deep breath in and out during each line because you are taking the words in and repelling any emotional or physical damage that you may have caused to your body. As you do this day to day, you are opening up your heart and bringing a new light to your body that has been hurt over the years. You will now realize how beautiful your body is and that you are enough despite what others may think of you. You are enough!

August 19, 2019

> And the time came when the risk to remain tight in a bud was more painful than the risk it took to blossom.
>
> —Anais Nin

Some of you may get exactly what this quote is saying, whereas others (aka my twin sister) are probably saying to yourself, "I don't get it." Well, Christina and the rest of the world, it refers to not having the courage to come out of our comfort zones and always being so afraid to face our fears. It is about closing yourself off from the endless possibilities that God has put right in front of you.

How does this resonate with me? It's fairly simple. I have always been afraid of life because my ego-minded self has been telling me to stay safe and play my cards low. However, after going to my guardian angel, Teresa (aka my spiritual healer), I have realized that with God lies no insecurities, no fear, no doubt, no lies, no regrets, and no challenges to overcome. Thus, I have started ascending myself to embrace and embark on a new journey of life that is unknown but truly worth walking into. I have decided to blossom myself in every situation that I come across, whether it is going to work, school, or a family event. I am going to show every single aspect of my well-being.

I can't begin to tell you the many times that I regret not being myself due to the fear of judgment and the pain I felt physically, emotionally, spiritually, and intellectually. I just wanted to break free and let the people I was with know who I was. This is one of most important secrets to finding your true happiness: free yourself to life. Please don't stop wasting your life like I have done for several years. The time is now to turn that rosebud into a majestic red rose.

Exercise

In order to accomplish this, I want you to write yourself a love letter starting with "Dear [insert your name]." Describe the things that you admire about yourself, that you honor yourself for, that you value yourself for, that you forgive yourself for, and that you thank yourself for. I want you to read this once a day to remind yourself of the endless qualities that you are capable of creating for yourself, and to remind yourself of who the real person is inside, instead of a persona that forgot about those amazing characteristics.

August 20, 2019

Dear Readers,

Unfortunately, the end is upon us. If you made it this far without crying, you deserve an Oscar. Regardless, the last action I wanted to make sure of before I ended this book is to donate. That is why I donated one hundred dollars to the CAM H Foundation in my honor, in order to help someone who is not yet a mental health survivor get the chance to be. I want to make it a mission of mine after this publication to ensure that all of you pay it forward in some way to those suffering from depression, anxiety, attempted suicide, or addiction. It doesn't even have to be a money donation; it can be something small, such as talking to someone you know. Remember, there are people struggling every day, and if we can save just one person, that's a blessing in itself.

To end off, the final prayer of this book is entitled "Peace."

Dear Heavenly Father,

I want to thank you for allowing me to have the emotional, spiritual, and intellectual power to create a book that will transform lives. I want to pray for all those suffering from mental illness and that you may provide them with the strength and courage to overcome their hardships. I want to pray for all of the doctors and research medical teams finding more ways and prescription medication to cure those with mental health issues. I want to pray for peace and serenity among all those who feel alone, and that you may provide them with the eyes to know that they are not alone. Above all, I pray for absolute peace on earth and upon every single human being so that people may live lives of no suffering.

Amen

Author's Note

I want to start off by saying thank you from the bottom of my heart for those who bought my book and for those who have contributed their real-life stories to it. Also, I want to say what a pleasure it has been going on this journey with you and sharing with you all my life struggles with mental health. In all honesty, I did question whether to publish this book due to the fact that I became very vulnerable in sharing my story. However, I do believe that I was meant to write this book so that I can stop the ongoing trauma that mental health is causing to humankind. Thus, I want you all to know that my mission to contribute to the mental health community does not stop here, and I will be donating (not only financially) to help as much as I can. I love you all. Remember that you hold the power to let yourself walk the path that you want your life to go. After all, whether you are my age, younger, or older, it's not about the destination—it's the journey that brought you to where you are now.

Printed in the United States
By Bookmasters